IF You Row, You Will Not Drift

IF You Row, You Will Not Drift

◆

Perfect Life Management – The Life Wizard

Manage Your Life Like a Professional Project Manager

Shaun H. Ajani

Writers Club Press

San Jose New York Lincoln Shanghai

IF You Row, You Will Not Drift
Perfect Life Management – The Life Wizard

Writers Club Press
an imprint of iUniverse, Inc.

For information address:
iUniverse, Inc.
5220 S. 16th St., Suite 200
Lincoln, NE 68512
www.iuniverse.com

ISBN: 0-595-24496-3

Printed in the United States of America

Manage Your Life Like a
Professional Project Manager

"The astronomer may speak to you of his understanding of space, but he cannot give you his understanding.
The musician may sing to you of the rhythm which is in all space, but he cannot give you the ear which arrests the rhythm nor the voice that echoes it.
And he who is versed in the science of numbers can tell of the regions of weight and measure, but he cannot conduct you thither.
For the vision of one man lends not its wings to another man."
—Khalil Gibral

"Order and structure to the reasons that border on the abstract and the conceptual...That is the secret of reality, the subsistence between nothing and something."
—Shaun H. Ajani

Contents

Preface

It happened to me one dark and snowy night in the mountains of New Mexico, while I was driving home, after a sixteen-hour day dispatching aircraft. It brushed my mind faintly. Maybe I decided to ignore it in some dark crevasse of my subconscious mind, or perhaps I was not ready to share it with the world at that time.

My thoughts ran thus:

We have methodology and tactics that go on forever, when it comes to work. We put in hours a day for others, *while our life suffers.*

We write, read, print, and scan till it gets dark outside, *while our life suffers.*

We come up with short cuts, budgets, meetings, and relationship builders for our co-workers, *while our life suffers.*

Why?

The answer that came to me was the fact that we are forced to *row,* while we are at work. But we seem to just *drift* in our personal day to day activities.

Let me be more precise. It is like going to the lake, getting in a row boat, and trying to reach the other side of the lake. We *know* that we want to reach the other shore, but we do not row, we just drift, we may finally get there, but we waste a lot of time, and are tremendously inefficient.

It seems against nature not to be efficient. But we humans have a way of defying logic and common sense, in the way we do things. Who knows exactly why we do the way we do things? Maybe we are just not motivated enough, or maybe we procrastinate, or maybe there is no boss telling us what to do, and when to do it. Whatever the case maybe, one thing is for sure. We do not take the time the effort to think out a proper methodology to take us through our daily lives. But the methodology exists, as it is evident from the corporate world.

What if we use these highly polished methodologies for our everyday lives? From making the budget for our next grocery list, to winning an argument on whether to buy that big screen TV, to setting effective goals?

A while ago, I wrote a quirky little book called, "Extreme Project Management". This book took the techniques and the methodology of traditional Project Management, of any commonplace corporate fortune 500 company, and seasoned it with unique and exclusively developed techniques to make the practice extremely effective. The newly evolved methodology took both the client and the Project Manager to great heights.

When we combine these vastly improved Management techniques with our daily activities, we create an unimaginable force that compel us to not only conceive and plan for things that we could not even imagine in our lives before, but accomplish these lofty goals in stride.

As I implemented this management philosophy to existence, my life went from living alone, a crazed and highly stressful life, in the isolated mountains of New Mexico, to being a very successful professional, and a happily married person, in the environment of my dreams. This is not because I was inept and indolent before, but because I just did not know how much a planned and managed approach can bring to our personal lives.

Of course, I did this transition in my mind, as I lived day by day, and perfected the system to be articulated to society. However, you have the advantage of being presented with a methodological and planned approach; The Life Wizard—Perfect Life Management.

We will take the management philosophies and methodology, and add material to it to reflect our daily lives, instead of corporate protocols. For example, instead of preparing a Cost and Benefit Analysis for a Policy Infrastructure Project, we will use the Cost and Benefit Analysis to show why we should purchase a new microwave oven.

Or instead of using the Risk Analysis for a new Web Site project, we will use Risk Analysis for our community affairs, or the family vacation. The same goes for budgets, new projects for home, purchases, reviews (of family members), marketing, task breakdown, and mediation. Can you imagine the benefits of not only to your immediate life, but also to those around you? Or if you have the inclination to be of the self-interested type, can you imagine acquiring virtually everything that you want in a family or a social setting? Where once you had to give in to the wishes of others.

Of course, not every coorporate methodology and processes are applicable. I have selected a few topics for assimilation with our life techniques. And I have adopted some to be more suitable to our needs. For example, my RABOHA (Review and Appraisal based on Human Attributes) has more then 40 different catogories that relates very specifically to the Manager-Employee relationship.

Hence, I changed it to RABOFA (Review and Appraisal based on Family Attributes). But I could not replace the catagories of employees with that of family members. It just did not make any sense. Therefore, the material changed significantly.

Speaking of family members. In order to use the methodology presented in Perfect Life Management, you must exercise them in all areas of your life, which is family, friends, and co-workers. I have used the "family" or "family members" as generic terms to represent your everyday life human contacs.

All things considered, the book represents a robust representation of how life can be run effeciently to maximize the incredible potantianal that we all possess.

As you embark on this new and exciting way of living, not everyone will embrace your new approach and design toward life. So remember this beautiful quote from Albert Einstein:

"Great spirits have always found violent opposition from mediocrity. The latter cannot understand it when a man does not thoughtlessly submit to hereditary prejudices but honestly and courageously uses his intelligence."

But like all great things, there is a small price. The price is humility. Let me explain...As you near the end of this book, you will know something. I do not mean that in an academic sense, but in a way, which is the truth. You will *know* that you are now able to acquire any objective, which passes you in everyday life. You will *know* because once you have read the Perfect Life Management in detail, you do not have to practice it. Just being aware of it will automatically arrange the details, to target your objective. You will have a sense of superiority like you have never even thought existed.

In a sort of a peculiar way, you will experience it from a third party's perspective, even your own actions, as if an invisible hand is guiding you.

If I may offer another enigma about the Perfect Life Manager, which will help you accomplish your final goal, or whatever you set your sights on. Every time you set out to execute the methodology by merely focusing on it, stop and ask yourself, "Will the outcome make everyone feel contented? Is it in the best interest of the general scheme of things? Or is it a mere selfish inclination"?

I am not saying that a little personal wish and fulfillment will negate Perfect Life Manager. But the outcome will be many times better, better then you initially set it out to be, if you partake in the above questions earnestly.

This is the Altruistic Qualifier. This may seem like a paradox, as on the one hand, we are trying to acquire goals and objectives for us, and surely that means that we will overrun some of the other's wishes. And on the other hand, we are being altruistic.

The answer lies in the very nature of the cooperation of others in attaining our objectives, conscious or unconscious. And because of the crucial nature of the Altruistic Qualifier, keep a check on it, throughout this program.

I know that you want things a bit clearer. Read on, and you will understand.

The Introduction

The learning process is not a random sequence of events that is learned by osmosis, by the author using a few anecdotes, which may have given the writer a passing fancy. A lot of writing has that contemporary theme, and we think that we can learn and apply the subject to our lives, and we live happily ever after.

Although, I would like to give some credit to the "sequence of events" method, where a series of scenarios are described, and the reader picks up on the idea, and subsequently learns. Hence, I have used the knowledge that I have acquired and analyzed during my intense private and professional life, as well have endeavored to juxtaposition the methodology that I wish to impart on you squarely on them.

This allows me the following logical approach. I will give you a cursory glance of what Project Management is, and to correspond that methodology to your private life, but not necessary in that clear-cut order. Due to the nature of the subject, which is the use of the methodology of corporate management practices in the everyday lives of the familiar individual, the *lessons* will have to come in an assortment of definitions, methodology, and life examples.

Basically, we will take the unique and highly effective methodology of Perfect Project Management and prime them on the best practices, and most acceptable Project Management methodology steps, such as:

- Requirements Gathering

- Analysis

- Budget

- Risk Management

- Work Break Down Structure (WBS)

- Scheduling and Closure

What can be a project? Well, a project can be anything, which has a beginning and an end. A project may also contain "Milestones", which are significant events in your project. You can pick an event, such as purchasing a home, or even just buying a microwave. Or you can pick a series of actions that you intend to do, and make it a project.

For example, I routinely designate my weekend daily activities as projects. The activities that I conducted on January 11, 2002, I designated it as "Project number 01-11-02". I continue my day, and use as many steps as I can use, as well as some of the technique to facilitate these steps, such as Critical Path Method, Reviews, and Appraisals.

It is very important to understand that you do not have to feel obligated to use all of these techniques and methodology presented in this book. You may only use whatever you feel comfortable with, and whichever you feel is of a realistic practice.

As you read further in the chapters, you will notice that I have not put forth the chapters in the order of the "acceptable Project Management methodology steps", as that would conflict with my objectives for this book. I have instead taken the Perfect Project Management principals, and used those principals to drive the logic of the book.

Of course, my objective, and the greatest desire, is not just the elucidation of Project Management, but also to embrace you, and guide you through the confusion of life, as a Life Manager…as a Life Wizard. Then delightfully that confusion will evolve to be a joyful example of orderliness.

As with any methodology, or a good idea, after completion of the presentation of such an event, it seems simple, even commonsensical, and that is the idea behind Life Wizardry, *it gives order and structure to the reasons that border on the abstract and the conceptual.* And hence, it gives order and structure to your life.

As you see the staunch structure of project Management listed, you will also see the sense and sagacity of applying the principals that drives that structure in our daily lives. Some of those principles are the unique methodology of Extreme Project Management that you will learn.

As we put this introductory chapter to rest, remember that there will be something required of you in this book. You will be obligated to extend yourself a bit to fully understand and utilize the Perfect Life Methodology. Maybe even extend yourself beyond your initial conception. One may wonder about how one can extend beyond which is the present comprehensible existence?

This may seem paradoxical at first, but I offer you to make an attempt to do so. Just the endeavor will make things possible. I would like to submit to you the possibility that everything that you will learn already rests in you, you can only be given a hint, a nudge, a presentation of the knowledge, and so you may finally consummate it.

Consider the words of Khalil Gibran from the "Prophet", which he wrote in 1923:

"No man can reveal to you aught but that which already lies half asleep in the dawning of our knowledge.

The teacher who walks in the shadow of the temple, among his followers, gives not of his wisdom but rather of his faith and his lovingness. If he is indeed wise he does not bid you enter the house of wisdom, but rather leads you to the threshold of your own mind."

One last thing…These principles are not just principles; they are elements of a philosophy, the philosophy of Perfect Life Management. As you go through the book, page after page, it will become clearer and clearer.

Positive Reciprocation

It is equally important to provide opinions, as it is to provide care; being careful, of course, that the end result is positive.

We are all blessed with family, friends, and co-workers that care for us. We wish to be equally considerate and useful to them. Positive Reciprocation is extremely sanctified part of our culture. It promotes goodwill and has a benevolence signature to it. As we march through life we learn and gain wisdom, which we wish to pass along.

In order for us to practice and maintain optimum Positive Reciprocation, we have to live efficient lives, so we have the maximum amount of time and influence. We all have a methodology, whether we know it or not, to live these efficient lives. But to be aware of that methodology, and continuously endeavor to attain greatness in it, takes us to an entirely different level. And with any new process, there are unfamiliar territories to traverse. You have probably heard it all your life that people don't like change. They resist it. They even fear it.

So in theory, due to Positive Reciprocation, at least initially, your friends and family might prevent you from using Perfect Life Manager. You can study the methodology and become a great success in life. But there are some consequences that will come along with the territory. Unfortunately, there will always be people, who will not understand, or will simply be behind the times. They will be unfamiliar with your methods, and in their haste of helpfulness to "set things straight", they may unintentionally interrupt your goals.

Some may be uninformed and somewhat imprudent, and will either be a hindrance in the big picture, or just downright insubordinate. Some will understand the value of what you are doing, but will have difficulty with the means of deployment, and will try and implement a self-governing and self-righteous remedy to neutralize any possible threat to his or her sense of regulatory order.

And, fortunately, some will have essentially good attitudes toward new ideas, which can benefit your life, or the family. You will most certainly find these superb agents to deploy the Perfect Life Management System.

As you practice Perfect Life Management, you will recognize your strengths and weaknesses. Your strengths will carry you over hurdles gracefully. On the other hand, you must beware of your weaknesses. You cannot be expected to overcome them by magic in a few days, but be watchful of them, and be positive if some well-meaning friend disparages your practice of being a Life Wizard.

Goal Manifestation

G oals are an ever-living reality in the corporate world. They besiege us. We have daily goals, weekly goals, monthly goals, yearly goals, and depending on the project you are on, even goals that stretch to the next five years. We make goals with the aid of project plans, schedulers, and personal digital assistance. In fact, we are quite good at it.

But what goals do you have for your personal life? If you have goals, is it just in your head? Or do you have a methodology to manifest them? This is one place where the exact superimposition of the techniques and tools of the cooperate world will not work. But the objective and the intention of reaching a goal, some goal, is certainly a thing to borrow from the business world.

Nothing significant will happen before you put down on paper your stated goals. You may have heard the word; or rather the concept of a goal, in many different forms. It may have come across to you in a multitude of appearances. You may have heard it called a goal, an ambition, a vision, a purpose, an intention, an aspiration, a dream, or you may plug in whatever your image of a desired end result you are trying to achieve. But let me restate that nothing significant will happen before you put down on paper your stated goals. It all starts from here.

We all live in immediate anguish. Pick up any picture of a successful person, and look closely. No matter what the future aspirations were, no matter how humble the beginnings were, no matter what the outlook may hold, the mind set of that person is immediate anguish.

There are two reasons for it. We do not keep good score to be thankful for the present, and we do not have clear goals. We do not treasure the past, or be hopeful of the future. For those who practice goal settings know exactly what I mean. Because you know where you have been; and more importantly, you know where you are going.

I have mentioned earlier that just a few years ago, I was living alone in the frozen mountains of New Mexico, while working long and hard hours. What I did not mention was that it was my intention, my goal to be in that exact position. You are probably thinking why would anybody what to live alone in the frozen mountain and work sixty hours a week? It was not that my goal was to "live alone in the frozen mountain and work sixty hours a week", but it was to:

1.   Have freedom

2.   Live an adventurous life in a wintry locale

3.   Live an audacious life in the mountains

4.   Be close to aviation

It was the collection, and the ultimate compilation, of my goals that I was manifesting!

Emerson once wrote, "The richest gifts we can bestow are the least marketable". Well, today, on this page, I am going to leave you with something that may not seem that significant or "marketable" at first, *but it will change the way you live, and continue to live in the future.*

You may choose, or not choose to read this chapter further. Because what you envision, what you manifest, will then be your responsibility, and may affect people outside your immediate self.

Grasp thoroughly the following pages of this section, for this is the crucial element of being a Life Wizard, of practicing Perfect Life Management.

The four goals that you see listed above were the only things I wanted in life, so I thought. Of course, I wanted freedom. I certainly got it. My intention toward that goal was so intense that every thing came together in my life to push me in that direction. I was in a position and location that prevented me from close contacts with family and friends.

I asked for freedom, but I did not ask for good relations with my family and friends.

I grew up in a tropical climate. The only time I saw snow was on television, or on vacations. I grew to adore the crisp tranquility after a fresh snowfall, the magnificence of a white wash, and the excitement of unimaginable cold snaps. So I wanted cold. I certainly got it. But combined with my other goal of freedom, I was put in a barren place, which was not exactly my dream location.

I asked for cold, but I did not ask for a village with friendly people.

Once again, growing up in a tropical climate, I was subjected to warm weather with unending plains and beaches. An ideal location to some but I longed for mountains. So I asked for mountains. I certainly got it. But it was the deserted brown mountains.

I asked for mountains, but I did not ask for the green mountains blessed with fertile lush.

And finally, was my dream goal of aviation. It was not just the airplanes, or the blue skies, but the actual action of aviation that seduced me. It called me so much that I gave up a good career for a few years just to dive in aviation, and quench my thirst. I asked for aviation, and I certainly got it! I got long hours of dispatching planes, spending ages in extreme stress, while the low-on-fuel planes circled snow bound small airports. Or planes calling with emergencies, or having a phone on each one of my ears, while two on hold with urgent calls from pilots and Air Traffic Control.

I asked for an aviation career, and but I did not ask for a fun job.

I thought I was skilled in goal setting. In fact I bragged about it, as most of my goals did manifest to reality. What I did not know was the incredible dynamics of goals, the astonishing power of the manifestation of the goals itself. What I learned was that I could not take goal setting lightly, nor will I let people I care about take it trivially. My goals did not just affect me, but also my friends and family.

GOAL MANIFESTATION DEVELOPMENT

Goal manifestation, by the way of goal setting, itself is very simple. In fact, so simple that it threw me for a very counterproductive loop for many years. I would advice you to study carefully the topics following the goal setting section, particularly those of Expectations and Status Reporting.

But let us not forget the message behind Perfect Life Management. We must study the methodology set aside for the corporate and business world, which we are trying to assimilate with our personal lives. Also, remember that as you help yourself, you will be helping your family and friends. You will raise them to the same pinnacle, as yourself. You will indeed be the Life Wizard.

But before we look a bit further in the Extreme Project Manager methodology, and how we use it for personal life, let me leave you with how I do goal setting.

First step: Simply envision the goal. When I say envision, I *mean* envision. For example, if your goal is to move into a new house by the middle of next year, then close your eyes and picture the house clearly. Do not make the same mistakes that I did. Be *specific*; for example, be specific about the neighborhood. If you have never been to that particular neighborhood or city, get a picture of it form the Internet, or a magazine.

Picture the interior

Picture the exterior

Picture the kitchen

Picture the front yard

Picture the back yard

As you read this, you will subconsciously summon images of your own ideal place.

Picture the garage

Picture the bedrooms

Picture the living room

Picture the study

Picture the sofas

Picture the table

Picture the chairs

Picture the carpet

Picture the wood floors

Picture the stairs

Picture the big screen television

Picture the stereo

Picture the DVD

Picture the fireplace

Picture the windows

Picture the doors

Picture the colors

Picture everything…Picture everything in detail!

And the smell…Imagine what everything would smell like! Can you smell your favorite food that you are cooking in your new huge kitchen? Can you smell the faint fragrance of the roses in the back yard through that open window? Can you get the soft whiff of the ocean as it roughly clashes on the rocks a few hundred feet from your balcony?

Can you hear it? Can you hear the ocean? Can you hear the pale, but the unmistakably robust sound of the waves? How about the sizzle of the food cooking right next to you?

Touch the leather on the recliner. Can you feel the abounding texture? Can you see the deep luxuriant color? Can you smell the plush tang of rich leather?

Feel your own presence. Feel how tremendously happy you are. Feel your heart beat a bit faster, as you see the bright kitchen again. Now much brighter then the first time you saw it. See about the room. Who is around you? Who *else* are you making happy?

You can peacefully come back to the present reality now. And that is all there is, this is the present reality, and what you experienced above is the future reality. They are both real, they are both true.

If you have trouble conjuring up images of your own creation, then you must spend more time dreaming about the things, which make you happy. Certainly, if you practice the above exercise again, you will see the difference. You may need some practice in conjuring up the future reality.

Second step: Write it down. Write it down in detail. Write it and read it. Read it every day. Here is a technique I use. Once a day, for about ten minutes I disappear from the world. I simply go to my car, read my goals, close my eyes, and live in my dream world for a while. It is incredibly empowering and inspiring.

How you acquire your objectives in not important, but the reasons you want to acquire them are. And the reasons are the feelings you create in yourself, when you envision your dreams so clearly. Everything in your life will be orchestrated to gently deliver you to your goals.

Do not forget those details that make the goals worth living. For example, just don't envision the house, envision it with the people you love and care for in it with you.

Once you have experienced the enchantment and the energy of having your goal manifested, you will only increase in frequency of having more and more goals pop up in your head, and in turn come true in the real world. That is the good news. The bad news is that if you have doubts, especially prolonged and persistent doubts about your goals and dreams from coming true, it will hold you back.

If you feel the goal manifestation idea to be somewhat insipid and wishy-washy, hold it back from others till you are convinced. But do not do yourself the injustice of being so cynical, as to not try it.

I had my doubts. But slowly as I conducted the goal manifestation process every time I thought of having something worthwhile in my life, the stronger my faith got. Perhaps it is the combination of vision, determination, and prayer. Or perhaps it is something so unexplained that the universe throws at us, which the humans cannot even conceive at the present time, but it works every time. Of course, it takes time, but eventually it works.

Be happy for the fact that you can use the goal manifestation process for even the smallest thing. Be even happier for the fact that once you get good at it, it is an automatic process.

Let me expound on what I mean by an automatic process.

A while back, I had a client, which was about 35 miles from my home. I knew that the drive commute, each way, would be at least an hour to an hour and a half, depending on the traffic. The problem was that I had some new goals for the subsequent three months, which were minor, but rather ambitions.

My goals were to read at least six books, accomplish a new significant self-improvement, and write for at least two hours a day. I felt that the time spent, and the fatigue inherited from this commute would put the manifestation of my goals in jeopardy.

I did not worry about it; I just left it to the creator and the creation to work it out.

Well, it turns out that during our next trip to the library that Saturday morning; I discovered a whole new section of audio books, which had evaded me before. In fact, I discovered a whole new library branch just around the corner from our house, which had audio books, such as the *unabridged* version of Napoleon Hill's "Think and Grow Rich", which I could not find anywhere else.

I also discovered vocabulary-building techniques that I could practice for just 15 minutes a night. And on top of all that, I somehow found the time, between relaxing fireside evenings and weekends to write for an average of two hours a night. And in combination with the many audio books that I found, I was able to "read" almost one book a week during my drives to the client site.

I learned that the end result may not be exactly the same, but it certainly is as potent, and just as magnificent and astonishing to the reasonable mind. Maybe it is explainable at some level, or maybe it is the charisma and exclusiveness of nature, which is just as unexplained and mysterious as nature itself. However you want to look at it, it works.

Write your goals down. These written goals will allow you to keep score and give you ample reasons to thank God for all your progress, and will provide you with a good road map for the future. I know that you will be successful.

CAUTION:

Before you begin the next few paragraphs on the "it" Paradox, I will caution you not to, unless you are in a relaxed and an open state of mind.

THE "IT" PARADOX

This section of the book will not be completed till I mention the "it" Paradox, which has preoccupied me for years. Just recently I have started to get a handle on it. Unfortunately it is not simple, but without experiencing it, you will not fully accomplish what you seek. And we all know, internally, what we seek.

As you read this, do not get discouraged, if you do not fully grasp the "it" Paradox. I do not expect you to. But when you finish this section of only a few hundred words, you will KNOW that you have understood something, which you did not before. Even that 5% to 10% understanding of the "it" will give you a feeling of silent strangeness.

The paradox I allude to is our purpose to reacquire what we never had. The paradox looses its potency, when I explain to you that you just think that you never had it. The "it" now becomes a mystery. The "it" I refer to is "us", or "you", in your case.

Stay with me for a few more minutes.

As you sit and read this, you have already begun to acquire "it". You will not fully realize this without preparation and practice. But you certainly will know that you have something more in your consciousness…something extra, by the time you finish reading this section on the "it" Paradox.

Stop everything for a moment, and take a look at your body. Look at your hands, your mid-section, your legs, turn your hands over to look at your palms. Now feel the inside of your body. You cannot perhaps *feel* it, so at least focus on it.

You know that brain you have inside your head? Focus on it, and acknowledge its existence. Chances are good that you have not had the opportunity to see your own brain, but I am sure that you know what your brain is *supposed* to look like. Picture your own brain in your mind. Now, if possible, picture whatever you can of the other parts of your internal organs. Focus on it, know it, and acknowledge its existence.

You know all the things that you just felt and acknowledged? That's not you.

What you were when you were ten years old, that's not you. What you were just a few months ago, before you added all that muscle by working out, or added all that fat by eating, is not you. That is the "it" Paradox. That is not you, or to be more precise, you are not what you think you are. You are the "it".

There is something else with you...There is something more then your body that you know so well.

If you follow the exercise from above once again, you will realize that there is this *other* self that was monitoring. That *other* self, that something more is the "it", that something more is you.

I know that you have not fully seized the "it" Paradox, but I also know that you have at least *felt* a fraction of the "it" Paradox by now.

As I began to realize the "it", during one of my meditation periods, I have never looked back. And neither will you. You have already come too far. It will only grow with you. And as it grows, it will be more powerful. And as it gets more powerful, everything you practiced in the previous section of Goals will be accomplished objectives for you.

This is not a book about meditation, or any other mind reflection. But if you ever feel compelled, take a few minutes and sit in peace and calm. Silence your mind, not just the outside world. And you will be able to experience the "it" more clearly.

When you feel like indulging in a bit more experimentation with the "it", go to a mirror, full length is the best choice. Make sure that there is nobody else in the room. Look at yourself. Look at yourself carefully. Look at yourself from a third person's perspective. You may have a difficult time doing this the first few times, but try. You will feel the presence of the "it".

THE "IT" AND TIME TRAVEL

Once I become more comfortable with the "it", I am able to do many things, which seems like something out of a fantasy movie. Recently, I stopped going for lunch, instead I go sit in my car, or anywhere that I can get some privacy, and close my eyes. I go through the dream manifestation process clearly. I see, I smell, I feel, and I encounter every infinitesimal moment of my future self. Quintessentially and characteristically, I *live* in the future. I make my "it" live in the future.

My "it" becomes the future!

Hence, for a minimum of half an hour a day, regardless of my present situation, I become the person, in a very real sense, of exactly what I want to be.

ANYTHING I WANT TO BE!

Recently, while having a conversion about Aristotle with a friend, the discussion came up about "matter". I started to think of the way matter changes shapes and forms. Think about it, the matter that makes up will be very different a year from now. A lot of which is "you" will not even exist. As you ingest, exist, and excrete, "your matter" is ever changing. Or rather ever "exchanging" with whatever that exists in the universe.

Hence, you will not be you. You will, in fact, be a different person. Realize this. Prepare for this. And willingly leave your limiting thoughts behind, and travel to the future with the new "it"; the "it" that has all your dreams and aspirations.

You can find half an hour a day to practice this. Whether you work or not, whether you are at home or traveling somewhere, whether you are doing great in life, or riddled with despondency, you can do this for half an hour a day. At first you do not have to involve the "it". But when you *send* the "it" in the future, the experience is more powerful, and hence the possibility of the fulfillment of your goals even more real.

And most importantly of all, it is not just that the experience is more powerful, but the experience is effectively a precursor and the blueprint to your future reality.

THE "IT" AND THE PARADOXICAL PRESENT

Another twist to the "it" and its relation to the Life Wizard version of time travel is the Paradoxical Present. A rather strange aspect of my writing must be explained to demonstrate this.

When I write, I almost never have the idea, as I write. The writing takes place in two phases. In phase one, the ideas come to me as I do my daily activities. The ideas pop in my head as I drive, eat, drink, play, and even sleep. I do not make an attempt to write them down in an orderly fashion. I may jot a word or two on a small scrap of paper. Just the act of writing starts something in my wits, which helps me later write literally thousands of words.

Phase two is when I actually sit in front of the keyboard to write. The words flow, as if from an unattended spout. But let me present here the strange part. As I sit back and review my work, after a couple of hours, usually a few typed pages, I discover to my bewilderment that I do not remember writing 90% of it.

I am more the reader, then the writer.

In fact, I do not even remember some of the words. I have to look them up in a dictionary! And they are perfect words, the most precise words that can exist in a sentence to flawlessly convey the exact truth. That is one of the reasons that I refuse to change most my words, even though they are sometimes difficult to understand for the average reader.

Who was writing? Of course, it was I, in the most logical sense. But who was *really* writing? The twists and turns of the paradoxical logic, which intertwines with the real self, the "it", the present, and the future can be perplexing, but rewarding to understand…If not understand, to be at least be aware of it; and if not aware, to just give it a glimpse. Whatever you do, you are already in the "it" orderliness. You have already done enough to get started.

In the above example, the "it" was somehow working with the my present self, as I drove, eat, drank, played, and slept, to ready me for the final transmutation of my future self. Hence, I existed in the present and the future at the same time. That is, the Paradoxical Present. This was the most joyful example of realizing the "it" for me. You, of course, will have the pick of the countless promises that exist for you.

The "it" will help you. The "it" is a lot more powerful, when it is realized to be present, then when it is realized as being absent. The "it" makes your willpower stronger, your determination more tenacious, and your dreams much more potent. The "it" gives purpose to life, and remains there long after you are dead.

Next time you are in doubt of your own significance, call up the "it", and you will be a believer. Perhaps "call up" is too pretentious of a term. *Realize* the "it".

Open your eyes, and look around. Seek out people, who have been enlightened. There are a lot more of these people then you think. Do not be fooled by their outward appearance, or their material possessions.

We all seek different things.

The "it" is elusive, but the "it" is not a secret. I do not have a name for it. Because if you know "it", you do not need a definition, and if you do not, then it defies definition.

If you feel as if you have had enough, you may stop here. Reflect on what you have learned, and then continue, when you feel comfortable.

Expectations

I f you have reflected on the past few pages, then I know that your
feverish desire to accomplish and realize your purpose is only
exceeded by your desire to help those you love achieve the same. There
are two tools, from the Perfect Life Management war chest, we will
deploy at this time, Expectation Escalation and Status Reports (we will
analyze this later in the book).

EXPECTATION ESCALATION

I have defined Expectation Escalation as, "reaching a state, where a
specified amount of work is completed to a superior quality in general,
than its preceding state, as a result of an optimistic objective." This
state will be dominant in your staff, in other words, your picked team
members.

As the Life Manager, or the Project Manager, of any particular
project that you are working on, you will always have the big picture.
You will have the best final estimates as a result of the input from many
different sources. Any *one* member on your team will not have the
complete picture, to ascertain the exact timeframe of a distinct compo-
nent of the project.

At this time, I would like to introduce another concept called, Pretense Irony, to help along in the Expectation Escalation process. In
Extreme Project Management, I have defined Pretense Irony as, "A circumstance, where one's superior knowledge and experience allows the
person to make a declaration, which may or may not reflect the actual
reality and fact of that particular timeline. At the same time making a
better decision, which is beneficial for the client, and other interested

parties, as well as fending off the competition, due to a more competitive forecast."

Meaning that if you take the Pretense Irony in account in the equation, it stands to reason that your staff (friends and family members); will not complete the project in time. However, as the goals of the timeline were somewhat embellished, the staff will not meet the goals, *but still achieve a higher goal then normal*, as the natural effort of the staff will be to meet the stated goal.

Another derivative of Expectation Escalation is the fact that you (the management) will discern their results as a success, even though the project staff did not meet the exact objectives. Your friends or family members, who are working with you, will appreciate that their genuine efforts were rewarded, and not just the *bottom line*. What is the big picture here? You have just created a more satisfied and indebted family members to you and any other stake holders in the project that you are trying to accomplish.

The very significant long term results of Expectation Escalation is that your team members, toward whom your allegiance lies to help, will ultimately be comfortable in having higher aspirations and goals then they were previously comfortable with.

THE EXPECTATION WIZARD

I would like to touch on something a bit more metaphysical for a moment. Not as a means of taking this book to a transcendental significance, but to establish a slightly different point of view of Expectation Escalation, and to reasonably validate it.

A curious thing happens when you believe in something. When you expect something to happen, it is as if by a force carved in us by some heavenly power manifests the expectation, or maneuvers us in the direction of the expectation. But the marvelous thing is that it seems to affect things that seemingly are beyond our control, even beyond our conception. I call it the Expectation Wizard.

I am sure you have experienced it countless times in your lives, but never really give it the attention it deserves, discounting the Expectation Wizard to a mere lucky break, or a creation of some other synchronized happenstance.

As we live out our lives, the Expectation Wizard pops in everywhere. It may visit us, during a relatively insignificant time, such as expecting slightly better results from our children's performance in school. Or the Wizard might shine at us at major events, such as a recovery from an illness of a loved one. But the ones we remember are the ones that may seem inconsequential to the outside world, but they are precious to us, as these are the visits of the Expectation Wizard that has shaped our beliefs.

I remember, quite a few years ago, when I was still in the process of comprehending my understanding of the wonderful world around me, and my sister Mehju was not yet five. My parents had taken us to a safari in the Wilpatu jungle in Sri Lanka. We were all very excited to see the famous leopards of Sri Lanka. In fact, there were amazing stories floating around about how aggressive the leopards were getting. My dad even arranged for an armed forester, in addition to the guide for our jeep, for the day of our safari into the jungle.

We all wanted to see the leopards, except for Mehju. She wanted to see monkeys. If truth be told, her anticipation was so pure that it was contagious. Pretty soon I was not only in anticipation of seeing monkeys, but quite expecting of them. I remember my parents also climbing aboard for the bandwagon.

Although, I suspect, their participation may have been purely to encourage our enthusiasm for our selected vacation.

It had become a happy monkey safari. We were talking monkeys all day. Monkeys were everywhere! Turn on the TV, and the monkeys were there. Open a magazine…and the monkeys were there.

Now just by itself, it taught me a great lesson about expectations. There is undoubtedly a certain power of manifestation here. But the Expectation Wizard continued on.

A few weeks later, we arrived in Colombo, the capital of Sri Lanka, late in the evening. We rented a cabana style hotel. I woke up the next morning with the aid of a combination of shrieks of delight and alarm. There, sitting on the ledge of the open window of our room, was a monkey! A monkey! On our windowsill! It continued on from there, in fact during our safari, we saw only three leopards (who seemed to be more scared of us, then we were of them), but we certainly saw hundreds of monkeys.

I ask you to trust the Expectation Wizard.

The year following our safari in the Wilpatu jungle, we found ourselves in an enjoyable vacation in Europe. There were about sixty of us. My dad, in his business minded inspiration, had arranged a group tour for several families, including us. We were flying, driving, and sailing all over Europe. We were intrigued by the historical shadow of Pompeii, graced by the elegant beauty of Rome, and dazzled by the well-dressed streets of Pairs.

But that is not what intrigued me. As you already know, I had an insatiable desire for aviation, even as a child. I was enthralled by every aspect of it. I begged and pleaded for a window seat at every departure. I savored and relished every moment of it.

The great thing was that I always got a window seat, regardless of the number of passengers on the flight, or the condition of our arrival; whether we were early, late, or on time. Once, the whole group got to the Geneva airport in Switzerland, in anticipation to fly to Amsterdam, Holland. To our disappointment, we discovered that the air career was having some serious problems, and could not provide us with the transportation. My dad made some quick deals, and got a charter flight from Basil, Switzerland.

The charter was a DC-9 cargo. We were informed that most of the seats did not have any windows, and there may be only a few in the whole plane, due to the cargo configuration. But of course, I knew that I would get a window seat.

It was time to board the plane. My heart skipped a beat with joy, when I saw that we were boarding the plane from the tail section. What an adventure! I was dizzy with delight, when I made my way up the stairs and emerged right next to the row that had the window!

I frantically scrapped my way in, threw my duffel bag on the luggage rack, and got comfortable in the window seat. As I watched the distant white capped mountains, and anticipated the glorious view of the Swiss Alps, my faith in the Expectation Wizard was strong.

Then came the test. One of my dad's assistants came running down the aisle, and said hurriedly, "Your mom wants to see you right away, grab your things, and come with me". There was urgency in his voice, which I could not snub.

This was quite a dilemma for me. Do I trust in my Expectation Wizard, and risk leaving this most wonderful seat? Or continue my claim on this gift that I had received for having faith in the Wizard? From the sound of his voice, I suspected that he was most interested in having me make a quick decision. I decided to take the leap of faith, and follow him up the aisle.

My expectations were high. It was high despite of the fact that all the evidence pointed to a possible outcome, which I did not look forward to. But that is the secret of the Wizard. To have high expectations, even higher then your logical mind leads you to believe.

I followed him, as we passed row after row with a frightening lack of windows. I tried to keep up, as he hurried on, surely provoked by the persuasive sounding broadcast by the Captain to take our seats, as we were gravely behind schedule.

Finally, he split opened a curtained area and beckoned me to enter. Imagine my beaming surprise, as I saw the grinning faces of my dad, mom, and sister comfortably seated in the fully windowed first class section of the plane. Not only did I have a window seat, but also I had the whole of the first class cabin at my disposal!

Many times we loose out on things, because we do not have enough faith. Remember, the small things that you gain from the trust, may be the ones that bond your faith; your faith in life, your faith in love, your faith in humanity, and your faith in God.

Till now you have seen some glimpses on how the methodology once held hostage by the corporate world can be entered in your personal life. As Expectation Escalation has no doubt demonstrated to you that you must fine-tune the methodology a little bit to fit the puzzle of own personal life project.

The Gathering

What is more vital then a blend of ideas within the loved few, whether it be friends or family? The initiative here is to provide something good, by the interaction and favor of thoughts and opinions. Walk down any corridor in the corporate world, and you will be met with at least a few conference rooms along the way. Not to mention the additional impromptu "meeting space", "meeting room", "meeting spot", and meeting this, or meeting that.

The fact of the matter is, even though our eyes close automatically in monotonous boredom, when we are captured and dragged into meetings, it is necessary. It is necessary to visualize, to create, to produce, and to capture the essence of the brainstorming group. No other discursive tool exists that is more functional.

However, to say that it is functional, as well as practical would be erroneous. We can take the major premise of assuming that meetings are functional, and we can take a minor premise to say that they are useful, but we cannot come to the conclusion that they are practical. The reason is the same as the filling of the inner recesses of the meeting. They are filled with humans. And they come in all different shapes, sizes, and temperament of intellect and disposition.

This is almost exactly true of any corporate environment. Fortunately, when it comes to arranging and carrying a gathering with your family and friends, it is a bit more practical. Hence, we may go as far as to say that the gatherings, or meetings, with friends and family are more functional *and* more practical, then those in the corporate environment.

We are already ahead of the game here, when you gather along with your friends and family to discuss an outcome. But the intentions of

having the meetings stay the same. It has been said before that it is necessary to have meetings to visualize, create, and to produce. It must also
be said then that the meetings can also be used for purposes beyond
that of the ordinary understanding of meetings. But in order to reap
the full endowment of meetings, you must understand in the dynamics
of running, maintenance, and objectives of the meetings.

Your final objectives are at stake here. The objectives can be the realization of a dream, or just the mobilization of a small project at home.
You may not have the complete control of the millions of variables that
will ultimately come together for the manifestation of your goals, but
you can facilitate, to the best of your abilities, the actions and the reac-
tions, which will make up the end result.

As you play the catalyst and the launching pad for these meetings,
be aware of the Custom Language that you possess and implement. It
does not matter whether you are reading this book in English, Spanish,
Chinese, Arabic, Urdu, Hindi, or French. Regardless of the language
you speak, every word you speak becomes a reality for somebody, and
eventually influences whatever, or whoever that steers the course to
your objectives.

YOUR CUSTOM LANGUAGE

Consider the following account that demonstrates the intricacies of the
Custom Language.

A few months ago, while working out of a cubicle, I overheard the
following conversation:

1st person: "Want to go to Caribou and get some coffee?"

2nd person: "No, I have too much work"

1st person: "Okay, then you can wither away and die"

I actually saw a vision of this poor person shriveled, dried-up, and dying. This, of course, happened without any interjection of my thoughts on purpose. You can say that it was automatic. I was amused by it, and consciously thought about it. But can you imagine some inadvertently spoken words that sends an image of such governance over someone's thoughts?

Hence, it is safe to say that pleasant words will promote pleasant visualization. And on the same train of logic, carefully sculptured words, will promote the desired visualization for the target receiver (person), and consequently the desired results.

LIFE MEETING MANAGEMENT

Most people do not consider it, but the first phase of any life management action begins with the involvement of the family members. Your family members are your project stakeholders. Make family gatherings, or meetings, a regular occurrence. In these meetings, you must establish yourself as the expert; in whatever the issues are in the family. Monitor the family closely to observe how they are reacting to your body language, adjust accordingly, but do not try and over interpret the family's body language.

We will cover the very important aspect of body language later. But first we must focus on the meeting itself. You can use many different techniques to sway the meeting your way. As you practice, you can even mix and match the different methods. The results will amaze you.

There are basically two kinds of meetings, the Kickoff Meeting, and the Process Meeting. The Kickoff meeting happens once, during the start of a project, while the Process meeting happens during the course of the project. As you read the methods I have provided for you below, here are the two crucial reasons that I think meetings are crucial to any undertaking:

1. *It establishes your role in the involvement in the project. For example, whom do you want to decide the next car for the family? How about the next vacation? What movies you watch? What you watch on TV? The ballet or the ball game?*

2. *It transcends the constraints of the conventional meetings, and extends in to the areas of your life, such as the idiosyncrasies of a particular social group, or your dealings with the particular constitutions of your co-workers.*

We will spotlight the following meeting methods:

- The Two Heads

- The Frame

- The Disappearance

- The Attendees

- Body Language

- Liquid Option

- Layered Agenda

THE TWO HEADS

One always thrives to be a better provider, or if your inclination is toward affection, then a better nurturer. In recent years, we have been endowed by the concept of synergy. Side Alpha—Side Bravo, or SASB uses synergy as the logical basis of argument.

SASB is based on the principle of "Two heads are better then one". I am sure you have heard this cliché countless time. SASB involves breaking up the team in two sides, and keeping them apart, during brainstorming sessions. This is truly designed to help your family come up with better ideas to a problem or a project that you are about to take on. This is true synergy in action. Even the simplest ideas can benefit the big picture.

SASB is powerful for the family unit, but its real energy can be felt when the project involves a slightly bigger crowd, such as a volunteer forum at the community center, or the PTA. The result of the SASB is not only that more ideas and solutions are generated, but also you are singled out as a leader, with genuinely unique leadership skills.

SASB authenticates a notion that there are only two sides, but in a tactical move, you may use many different options. For example Side Alpha—Side Bravo can easily be Side Alpha—Side Bravo—Side Charlie—Side Delta—Side Echo, and so on.

There is a clandestine side of SASB, as well. In a smaller gathering, you can instill this methodology without the knowledge of the participants by merely taking a couple of people aside, and asking them a couple of key questions. This also gives you a greater opportunity to manipulate the final decision. For example, on a recent visit to California, our group was undecided, as is the case with many outings with friends, to our final destination and entertainment for that evening.

Most of the guys were flirting with the idea of a quite evening in Marina Del Ray, while the audacious some were contemplating on jumping on the night flight to San Francisco, to have dinner on the Fisherman's Warf. I, on the other hand, was leaning toward a healthier outcome, particularly a hike in the Santa Monica Mountains. Normally, I would have given in to the majority and spent the evening relaxing in the marina. But I was armed with SASB, and was in anticipation of firing it.

However, at the same time, I did not want to discount any other ideas that may be lingering in some other minds. *To outwardly discuss our options with everyone at the same time, those weaker ideas may never be heard.* I was certainly open to suggestions, in order to optimize my trip to the Golden State. This was the perfect opportunity for SASB. I accomplished two main goals:

- First, it gave me the opportunity to hear all ideas

- And second, it gave me the opening to steer any ideas that I liked my way

By quietly interviewing all my friends, and hearing all their *sides*, I decided that the flight to San Francisco was definitely a more exciting option, and was able to implement it successfully.

THE FRAME

Indeed, it is the wish of all beings to have a sense of self-importance. But self-importance without purpose is irrefutably a squander. Hence, there is another view needed for this subject matter.

Time/Importance Framing (TIF) is an event that occurs when a family member, or a friend, looks at you with a TIF level, which is slightly higher, then the normal TIF. A TIF level is basically a point of reference that we use to judge the importance we give to people, right before acting in favor of, or against that person.

For example, if a family member asks you to attend a discussion, you will go through a thought process, containing of several different criteria that you will use to decide on the action. We always tend to give importance to things in our own priorities, which may, or may not, be beneficial for that particular happenstance. TIF balances those priorities.

If you think that the family member requesting your input has enough value to offer you, you will probably accept the offer to meet. And depending on how much you value the person's TIF, you will decide on other factors as well. For example, how much time are you willing to spend on this event? How prone are you to cancel your appointment with the family member? And so on. It is very important to understand this concept, as not only your family members, but also everyone else around you is constantly using TIF.

In essence, we are changing the *Perceptive Reality* of these people. I introduced an intriguing theory on *Perceptive Reality* in my short story that I wrote with Jeremy Bierly, "The Eternal Optimist". It will be beneficial to give it a cursory glance. Here is an excerpt from it:

"People tend to move toward the reality that makes them happy…I have introduced, in the Eternal Optimist, my theory of the *Realm of Perceptive Reality* (RPR). RPR has been whirling around in my mind for some years now; finally I have the chance to articulate it.

*It is based on the very correct premise that there is one, **and only one**, true reality that exists in the universe. And in its most fundamental form, RPR is that perception of reality, which we gather and exist in, from **that** one true reality.*"

Please understand that TIF is not there to create a counterfeit image for you. We are changing the perceptive reality of these people, and are helping them put our time and importance in the right frame of reference to produce the most efficient results for the family. Following are some of the gears that make TIF work:

THE DISAPPEARANCE

For your family to form a positive TIF level, you must display that your time is valuable, and that you are important. Choose a recurrent gathering, such as a Family Status Meeting (covered later), so all the regular family members are present. Around ten minutes or so in the meeting (to ensure everyone is present), announce in a casual way that you have to leave early for another task, such as making an important phone call to someone else.

Do not explain, at the time, with whom, for what, or give any other details. Give the appearance that you have places to go, and people to see, which are occupying your very busy schedule.

This works very well at all levels; for example, if you are getting together with a bunch of friends over the weekend, or if you are out for dinner with co-workers.

While exercising the "departure" sequence, ensure that you take everyone's feelings in account. Your objective is to increase your TIF level, not to decrease the self-image of your friends and family. This takes practice, but it is very effective.

THE ATTENDEES

Include the world of your family and friends with you, when you make important decisions, whether it is buying a new automobile, painting the doors in the foyer, or upgrading that screeching furnace. They will help you decide better, and interject more ideas. But be realistic in the people you invite, lest you open the doors for those who will hinder your objectives.

If this is to be a brainstorming, or solutions planning session, then feel free to invite all. Participation is wonderful and harmonious amongst friends and family. If you have a big family or a group of people, include only the "team leads". Those who you mean to give the main responsibilities, to carry the project forward.

Take the case of painting the doors in a part of your house. Let us assume that you have at your disposal a staff of ten team members, three kids, six of their friends, and a husband. You may allocate the husband the duty of purchasing and transporting the painting supplies, while you may delegate one of the older kids, as the "Team Lead" in the actual painting of the doors, while you act as the "Project Director".

During the initial meeting, or the "Project Kick-off" meeting, you may only invite the Team Leads, which in this case, include the designated team lead of the painting team, and your husband. This may seem like quite a benign example of a project, but consider the amount of complications by having too many attendees.

You may have a certain color in mind, and the exact number of doors, which need to be painted. I can guarantee that if you invite every team member to the meeting, someone will suggest, "why don't you just paint all of the doors?" And the next thing you know, some one else might run with that idea, or even suggest something else. You may have a number of reasons to consider only a particular number of doors, or a particular color, which you do not need to, or cannot explain to others. For example, there may be a lack of money for the project.

Give everyone a fair chance. But in your reasonable opinion, if the project has a low significant value in how it will ultimately affect your family, then limit the invitees.

BODY LANGUAGE

How acutely depleted we would be in our understanding of the present world, if we chased after meanings in people's body language, knowing well that in today's exposure to globalization, "body language" just does not have the same reliability, as it did in the past.

I am certainly not big on body language. Although, it is more reliable within family and friends, as the cross-cultural differences within this group are limited. But you need to be aware of body language. At least, consider two things. How *not* to misinterpret body language, and how *not* to be misunderstood.

Here is a story that I often relay to illustrate my point:

A few years ago, I had the unfortunate opportunity of being taken into for questioning by some very sinister looking Russian officials, at a Russian airport. I was the only American flying from a small airport in Moscow to Alaska, and some unscrupulous Russian officials had picked me out.

I sat in a barely furnished room. I did not speak a word of Russian (except being able to ask for the bathroom) and they did not speak a word of English. All they said was, "problem", and all I kept repeating was, "no, no problem".

All I could see was four Russian guards in uniform looking at me, and talking amongst themselves in humorless tones. By reading their body language I could *tell* that they wanted something *big* from me. And after hearing a lot of stories from other travelers, I knew it was money.

They were able to locate a Bulgarian, who spoke English. He exchanged a few words with the Russians for a while, and as I had suspected, he indicated that they knew that I lived in San Francisco, and was carrying US Dollars.

I was carrying around $600, and would have gladly shared it with them. Except for one thing, I do not offer bribes, and I certainly was not going to be strong-armed into it. After watching a lot of James Bond movies in my lifetime, I *assumed* that the Russians had read that in *my* body language, and were determined to break me, especially with my flight leaving within the hour. Finally, the Bulgarian told me the amount the Russians were demanding. It was just $25!

From a postmortem of the story, I experienced the following very important revelation. I *did* read their body well. They *did* want something valuable from me. That is valuable to *them*, not me. Given the economy of Russia, I am able to conclude that $25 is well worth it for them to put me through a harrowing experience. It is not just a matter of reading the body language, but one of reading their minds, which I must say, is quite impossible for me at this time.

Attempting to read body language puts us in more of a communications conundrum, then if we were to concentrate on the actual subject being discussed.

As I mentioned earlier, there are two basic things to consider here, how *not* to misinterpret body language, and how *not* to be misunderstood. Hence, there still remains the matter of *not* being misunderstood.

Do not care whether the family member is folding his arms, or scratching his nose, or looking out the window. But do care about how *you* appear. Ensure that you appear completely neutral and interested.

For example, I always sit close to the table, slightly leaning forward, with both my arms on the table, either taking notes or slightly touching my hands at the figure tips. Look directly at the person talking, and nod occasionally, and you will be amazed, how well the meeting will go.

Even among the family members and friends, you will gain more respect, as time goes forward, for being more attentive to others. They will credit you with listening and caring, even if that is not your main objective.

LIQUID OPTION

I expect that Liquid Option is a good title for this short section, as it accounts two things. The fact that the *matter* liquid is involved that I found to be so effective in this particular short-term tactical objective, and that that it implies a certain flow, as in the case of the passage of time.

LIQUID FIRST

This revelation was painfully bestowed upon me recently, as I found myself in a meeting with a tearing desire to shoot for the bathroom. The cause of such an effect was an over indulgence in liquid; particularly, after consuming mass quantities of black coffee during the first hour of the two-hour meeting. At this point, I had the realization of the power of liquid.

This method is slightly unhallowed, yet quite effective, as a short-range tactical move. If you want to keep a meeting short, lavish your team members with plenty of coffee, tea, water, juices, and anything that *flows*, about half an hour *before* the meeting. Fifteen or so minutes after the meeting commences, your team members will be jittery and willing to conclude the meeting, even compromise their positions.

TIME AND FUNCTION

This leads us to a slightly more complicated matter of Time and Function. I say Time and Function, because I have never been able to perceive time on its own. Sometimes fifteen minutes seems like half an hour, and half an hour seems more like fifteen minutes. This of course, directly correlates with the function that I am performing.

When I am watching my favorite shows, such as Star Trek and The Simpsons, time certainly seems to travel quickly. Certainly, a good episode of Star Trek, which should take 60 minutes, seems more like 40, and even less for those particularly exciting episodes. And ditto for The Simpsons, or for that matter, any activity that I am enjoying.

The converse is unquestionably true, as well. If I am watching, or doing, something, which to my mind is remarkably boring, an hour seems like a lot more. There is not a single human being that has not experienced this phenomenon. The phenomenon is definitely common, and I want you to be conscious and insightful of the fact that it ties with the Liquid Option above.

It is certain that the people in the above meeting, who are suffering from the case of the desire of an early departure, and the desperation of an early conclusion of the meeting, experience a slower passage of time, then those who are unaffected.

This is also the time and the opportunity to take in account of any other external stimuli or motivation that you can design, which would speed up, or slow down time for your chosen few.

LAYERED AGENDA

The delicious pungent aroma of an onion inspired the creation of the Layered Agenda. It is like an onion. It benefits from an outer layer, which you will expose to the family members, and you will be in complete control on how many layers you want to peel off.

Another analogy is a book's table of content. The members are exposed to the chapter titles, only if time permits, and if you so wish, you may dive deeper in each topic, or you may not. This gives you not only complete control of the meeting topics, but also what you want the others to see, and what you do not want them to see.

For example, here is a Layered Agenda for a trip I was planning for the summer of 2001:

Here is a good visual for how the Layered Agenda can work:

1. Egypt

    1.1. Cairo visit

        1.1.1. Pyramid tour

            1.1.1.1. Inside the Pyramid visit

        1.1.2. Egyptian Museum

        1.1.3. Nile

            1.1.3.1. Dinner on the Nile

            1.1.3.2. Hotel on the Nile

    1.2. Luxor visit

        1.2.1. Train to Luxor

            1.2.1.1. Security concerns

2. Journey

    2.1. Airlines

        2.1.1. Economy

        2.1.2. First Class option

            2.1.2.1. Frequent flyer miles option

3. Hotel

3.1. Marriott

3.2. Inter-Continental

The Layered Agenda lets you reserve the right to a decision, if you play your cards correctly. By the way, our vacation was great!

For example, in this case, my wife shares my love for ancient Egyptian artifacts; our house is a monument to them. But can you see how I may have reserved certain decision rights? I may have want to fly first class, and not have chosen to peel that particular layer, thus limiting my conversation to just the airlines. Or I may have the inclination toward the Marriott, which is practically an oasis in the desert, or the Egyptian Museum, or the cruise on the Nile, or…Well, you see where I am going with this.

Practice the layer…It will benefit you.

You will become comfortable with the deployment of one of the techniques that you have just been exposed to. But practice as many as you can, you will get more confidence in using them. You have surely used some or all of the gathering methodology in your lifetime. But having a realization of their existence gives the whole meeting scenario organization and structure.

As we wrap up the meeting section, consider this. There will always be two kinds of elements in the meetings. One will constitute the idea part, where things and thoughts are created. At most times, this will be you, the Life Manager. However, you will need the help of the other part, which constitutes the builders of these ideas. Something has to happen on the other end to realize any idea, dream, or objective.

The two main objectives of the meeting, the establishment of your involvement, and the level of possible administration and the management of the group, based on their respective idiosyncrasies, must always be with you.

The Specialist

Nothing is sweeter to a person then hearing that you are an expert at something they need solved. One good thing about being a Life Manager is that you do not have to be an expert particularly at anything specific, just know Life Management. As a skilled Perfect Life Manager, you will pick out the expert people, who will populate your project, and you will share the credit for it.

For example, it is time to buy a new car. You want to ensure that the car is a nice sporty SUV, and not a lumpy station wagon. And you know just the right person to pick (populate your project) to help you acquire this objective. For example, you have two kids and a husband to deal with. If kid number one likes lumpy station wagons, then it will be prudent to pick kid number two instead, to assist you in planning and purchasing the car.

Declaring yourself a specialist for the job is simple.

First, just ask the right questions to determine exactly what the family needs help with. For example, is your husband too busy to take the time out to go look for the car? Well, amazingly enough, this will be the week that you have the *extra* time on your hands to go from dealer to dealer to search for that perfect car.

Second, make a mental note to pick the right person on your team, or if the family is assigning the team, ensure that you specifically ask for that particular skill. Make a point to remind the family that it is a crucial skill. And third, quickly mention to the family a past experience (a vague far off place), even if it is *not* exactly the same circumstance, where you successfully collaborated to solve a similar problem.

Nobody expects you to be the perfect authority; they just want reassurances that you will attain the objective to everyone's satisfaction.

According to the Extreme Project Manager, in the corporate arena, "the professional world is besieged with people, who declare themselves as an expert in something. And if this is carried out with enough self-assurance, the mass will believe it. Just walk into any bookstore and you will be inundated with books, tapes, and videos of these experts introducing new programs and courses. When enough faith is put in these experts, changes *do* happen. Hence, it is not the actual ability and the skills of the expert, but of the person receiving it.

Your objective is to deliver this image in such a way that the client, or your audience, will put their trust in you. The great thing about this is that with the right staff and little knowledge, you can pull this off successfully."

Remember that you have to protect your image as the specialist. Do not let your team members intimidate you. The strategy is to project the same expert image, at the same time be able to use the team member's expertise for the advantage of the project. It is acceptable to disclose to the team member that your expertise lies in more of an abstract form, needed to run the project. However, there may be certain tasks that will need the "particular expertise" of that team member.

For example, you may not know enough about engines. Recently I was looking for a Toyota Land Cruiser. The sales person said that it came with a 230-hp 32-valve V8 engine. Considering that I can hardly tell the difference between a sedan and an SUV, I certainly was not a specialist for purchasing that particular automobile.

However, by having my friend Bob on the team, I could have used his expert knowledge of cars engines, and have been a successful project manager for the purchase of the Land Cruiser. In other words, even though in reality I was clearly not an expert in the lower objective of "analyzing the engine", I could still be a specialist in the higher objective of "purchasing of the car".

Sir Isaac Newton once said, "If I have seen further it is by standing on the shoulders of giants."

Use the opportunity of having people smarter then you on the team to further yourself. You do not have to be the best in everything. In fact, if you try to project that image, your own team members will quickly mark you as a charlatan, and you will be less effective for your family.

Status Report

A s a Perfect Life Manager, you must attain and maintain the larger picture of Expectation Escalation. In most management best practices, one of the most popular ways to keep track of the project is a Status Report. To escalate the expectation, Status Reports are great conduits. It declares to the members what achievements you expect from them every week.

We must not deviate too much from the look and feel of the Extreme Project Management. After all, that is what inspired me to introduce Perfect Life Management to the world. From the Extreme Project Management view, the following is perceived on Status Reports:

"It seems as if complexity in a project is inversely proportional to Status Reports. As things get complicated in the workplace, both in methodology and technology, Status Reports get simpler. Either the Project Managers, or the team leads, do not want to be bothered with the avalanche of information, or just do not understand the content. Either way, it is okay. As the Project Manager, one does not have to study every molecule of information.

By giving the impression that information is not necessarily needed in the Status Reports, a manager erroneously sends out the signal that the information is not significant. Nothing could be farther from the truth. Even if the manager does not fully understand the material, it is important to have that information, more so for the person making the report, then the Project Manager."

Can you picture a project at home, which might desire your interest but concede to your inexpertness? Recently, after a particularly cold snap, our garage door refused to submit to our request for it to open.

Turns out that the remote control was somehow interfering with the signal, and we had to disconnect it for the door to open. As a matter of fact, as I write this sentence that drama is unfolding!

To start with, I cannot possibly fix the garage door, I am just not mechanically inclined, and my forte lies elsewhere. Now you may be the one to pick up the spanner and go to work, but for this case lets assume that you do not have the inclination to play the handy man.

As a Project Manager, I will decide not to actually participate in the gritty details of planning of the repair, but I certainly will be big enough to give them a hand in the mending process. This departures greatly from the corporate management style, where the Project Manager will almost never participate in the labor.

In this case, I will ensure that I control the big picture by coordinating things like purchasing the supplies, researching and buying the source documentation to fix a garage door, arranging the food and drinks, and basically playing the host and the facilitator. And to top it all off, I will prepare a Status Report template and assist the workers to fill it out to ensure three main purposes:

1. An aggregate and summative control of the project

2. To project the *look & feel* of a Project Manager

3. To politically win over the friends and family members by showing that you are acutely interested, and what they are doing is indeed significant

Also keep in mind that we are selecting a rather difficult project and it ties in to the actual word "project". Perfect Life Management applies to all aspects of life's projects, from washing dishes to making a budget, as this will become clearer to you later in the book, when we indulge in topics like Task Breakdown and Budget issues.

Of course, a simple task like washing dishes will benefit less from Status Reports, unless it is condensed in a bigger project. For example, you could have a project called. "House Chores"; nevertheless, as this opportunity has so graciously presented itself to us, we will use the "Garage Door Project" to illustrate Status Reports.

It will be beneficial to take a closer look at Status Reports. Lets revert back to the corporate world for a moment, and consider the average Status Report prepared by a team lead on a typical project. It includes the following information:

Typical Status Report:

From: Will Worker

To: Mike Manager

Date: Ending Week December 28, 2001

Work in Progress:

Gathered work requirements

Scheduled tasks

Work Planned:

Assign work to appropriate worker

Continue quality assurance tasks

Comments:

Taking day off on the first of January

The above Status Report is a very normal representation of a typical project. It demands bland and lackluster information from the team members.

An alternative Status Report, which we will be using for the Life Management, can demand more robust information, forcibly throwing the report maker in the midst of the subjects being discussed, as well as giving the team member a little more feeling of substance. The report can also be shared between team members to generate a more hearty understanding of the subject and the crux of the project.

Here is an alternate report:

From: Larry Leader

To: Mike Manager

Date: Ending December 10, 2001

Describe Accomplishments this Week:

Describe any Concerns or Issues:

Describe Plans for Next Week:

Message for the Team:

Attachments to Support this Report:

By proclaiming work as "accomplishments", you are generating a positive mental image on the work done this week by the team members. Other attributes, such as providing more space for the team member to put the thoughts down and giving the Status Report the look and feel of a "report", will help your cause as well.

REQUIREMENTS

With the creation of any Status Report, the maker of the report indirectly reports on the requirements being attained. Hence, this would be a good time to take a closer look at requirements.

In any project, the first step is always to identify the requirements. These are essentially the success criteria. We can identify the requirements for the Garage Door Project:

- Garage door must open by remote control

- Garage door must open with the same speed as the original one

- Garage door must have an aesthetic appearance

- Garage door must be completed by the end of January

- Garage door must be completed with the provided parts and tools

You must take a good look at the requirements, and identify risks and assumptions. We will certainly spend a few pages discussing that later in the book.

Next, the whole project must be broken down into smaller manageable tasks. This is called a Work Breakdown Structure (WBS). We will spend considerable time on it, as well.

Now the time comes to allocate the tasks to the resources. The resources can be the people that you will be using, or the tools that will be used. Of course, the resources require money, and that requires a budget. We will spend some time on budgets also.

Once you have all your ducks in line, then you can initiate the project. Your objective is to meet your original requirements.

Although, this has been a great example, I wish to hasten my departure from the Garage Door project. After all, the whole idea of the book is the managing of the life, and the preceding project was a "project" in very real terms, as perhaps seen by professional Project

Managers. But I decided that it would benefit the bigger cause, hence my use of the Garage Door project. Let us not speak of it again!

Of course, it would be great practice, if not entertaining, to try this on a more unsophisticated task. Imagine that you have allocated the dishwashing chore as the Dish and Utensil Reallocation Project (DURP). You have allocated three family members to the Project DRUP. You may, or may not be part of it.

Member number one has Mondays, Wednesdays, and Thursdays. Member number two has Tuesdays, Fridays, and Sundays. Lets assume that you will eat out on Saturdays. Member number three will be the project lead on week one. You will rotate team leadership every two weeks. Hence, the DURP team will get new leadership fortnightly. The team leads will file the Status Reports.

Just for practice, can you identify the possible requirements in DURP? Here are some hints:

- Level of dryness in the end product

- Storage place (on the counter? Or in the cabinets?)

- Level of cleansing (Just rinse and put in the dishwasher? Or complete washing of the dishes?)

So what accomplishment can DURP have? It seems like such a basic *no-brainer* project. If the family members are young, it will give them a sense of purpose and completion for a task. They will feel recognized for doing a household chore.

By inviting them to share any concerns, comments, or issues freely, they will feel heard, and ultimately satisfied. Although, I am targeting the younger members of the family here, low level chores can be good practice to set the mood and tone for an organized life.

It also gives good practice in using other members of the family in productive tasks. You may exercise increasing the bar every few weeks, to practice Expectation Escalation.

For example, give a time limit for the task, or set a deadline for it to be completed. Encourage the members from coming up with better ideas to do a task. For example, can the configuration of the kitchen be changed for more efficiency or safety?

This Status Report also hints, under the "Message for the Team" section, that all the team members will share the report. This encourages the report writer to not only voice special concerns, but to distribute any other information that may be helpful to the other team leads in completing the project.

The sharing of information will open trust barriers, and will give you an invaluable insight to the interaction and social interfacing within your family unit, or friend circle.

Finally, this kind of report clearly offers to accept any attachments to go along with the accomplishments of the week. For example, if there is a dispute about certain breakage in the dishwashing function, an explanation can be attached.

Can you see the immense influence of such training for kids growing up? Or even husband and wife team doing this? The actual and literal of just one project, such as DURP may seem totally insignificant, even comical, but do not let that delude you.

There is another aspect of Status Reports that takes an even more personal look in the help of analyzing your life, and ultimately help you do better Life Management. It is the Personal Status Report, as discussed in the following section.

PERSONAL STATUS

Setting things aside of the projects, I have found vast rewards and advantages in maintaining a Personal Status Report for everyday activities, which I file to myself, or another family member each Friday afternoon. For example, I use a simple Status Report, which includes:

• Current Achievements

- Plans for Next Week

- Concerns and Issues

I give the Personal Status Report a look, which is separate and distinct from the Status Report that I use for the projects at home. For example, I tend to hand write the Personal Status Report, and file it away. And I limit it to the above three categories.

For example, below is a typical Personal Status Report:

Current Achievements:

Wrote five pages of the new book

Able to attend gym three times

Prepared a new method of priming firewood

Plans for Next Week:

Continue writing the new book

Wake up at 5 AM every morning for the gym

Start the "salads only for dinner" diet

Stock up pantry for the next three weeks

Issues and Concerns:

Over 37 rejections for the next book already, change of approach is needed

Knee pain acting up again

It is quite astounding how unbelievably effective a Personal Status Report can be in your life, and how accommodating it is for any future plans. This can also take place of a simple journal or a diary. I find it to be a refreshing scorecard for me, when I visit my old status reports after a few months.

These little actions set in motion incredible momentum that carries you to do similar powerful organizational tasks for the more important things in life. For example, applying for a home loan (if you have done that, you know that could be a huge project), planning a vacation, searching for a better job, or even starting a new business.

The Logic of Truth

I have heard too many times the trite, hackneyed, and worn-out cli-
chés about telling the truth. We have been bombarded with narra-
tives from religious books, to anecdote of leaders and ancient figures
that stir emotions in us, and have been used to display the significance
of truth.

It has also been made quite clear to us the distasteful penalties of
falsehood and pretense. You get terminated from work, shunned by
friends, and risk of acquiring an unhealthy reputation amongst your
peers. But in spite of all this do you think that you can safely maneuver
in any activity without the benefit of encountering a lie? Whether it
may be you not telling the truth, or someone else telling you a lie.

If by now you are assuming that I am about to compel you in any
way to lie to your friends and family, then your assumption is erroneous. I merely want you to have an awareness of the fact that the truth is
not quite the truth.

Allow me to elucidate. The truth to you is not quite the truth to the
other person. To be more precise, the truth to you may not be perceived as the truth to the other person. We briefly touched on the
Realm of Perceptive Reality (RPR) earlier. RPR is based on the true reality, which exist in the universe, and how it relates to our personal RPR.
What I am referring to here is somewhat related to RPR, but it does
not have the impression of wholeness to it.

We can start by trying to define to what truth is. But I am sure that
you would appreciate if I keep the general sense of the discussion con-
fined to Project Management, or Life Management. Once again, we
are not trying to validate the reason behind the virtue and vice of truth

or falsehood. We want to briefly explore what you may encounter in a conceptual sense.

Truth, in management, is what is NOT false. What you think of as "yes" in your mind, but express it as a "maybe" is not false, but is close enough to truth. And if a "yes" to a "maybe" is acceptable, then a "maybe" to a "no" can be acceptable also.

But do no make the mistake of applying the associative property in logic of:

IF A = B, And B = C, THEN A = C.

Or A = B = C, in other words assuming that if "yes" is okay, and "maybe" is okay, then it must be okay to convert a "yes" to a "no". That is definitely not the truth.

Once an associate asked me what time the flight was. Knowing that he is usually late, I indicated that it was "maybe on time. But we should hurry, lest we should miss the flight". I indicated the "maybe" although I knew that the flight was on time. I converted the "yes" in my mind to a "maybe" outwardly.

As you become aware of the smallest nuances of the shifts in language to acquire a purpose in management, you realize that truth is a prevailing force in all things that are good. But the main idea is to use the truth in the sense of the greater good, and in having decided that, it is quite endurable for even the pious few to accept the variation of the truth for the purpose of management.

Risk Equalizer

Attach the concept of risk to anything, and you will surely be dragged into a melancholy disposition, or to the least, experience a bit of anxiety. Risk is something to respond to, even plan for, and certainly not react to. This is true for almost all instances of projects, which are initiated, but it only applies to certain cases in your everyday life. For example, projects (you must practice looking at everything as a project) that you may be involved in outside of your immediate home.

Just like a project manager, when you walk up to a situation that already exists, there may be certain pre-conditions present, which may affect the outcome of your objectives. And then there may be conditions that may come up at a later time, given the environment, which may affect your objectives. These pre-existing conditions are the "assumptions", and the "conditions that may come up at a later time" are the risks.

I feel as if the risks are really collections of loose ends. Assumptions are not so bad, as you already know that they exist, and more importantly, as they were there before you got involved, it is really "not your fault". Assumptions may still affect your final objectives, but at least, the stigma attached to them, if you fail, is not as great.

You are then the effect, and not the cause. Hence, it stands to reason that it is to your benefit, if you have more assumptions then risks. And it makes even more sense, if you could convert some of those risks to assumptions.

Consider my theory on risk Equalization:

"Risk Equalizer is an action point that challenges risks defined by the project, and converts them to assumptions, by assigning each pre-defined risk a responsibility, then assigning new risks, with improved net effect."

The idea here is to have risks that are slightly more in your control. When you approach any outside project, you will encounter risks. Every risk must have a remedy, even if it sounds improbable. If you cannot find reasonable remedies to risks, you might want to reconsider getting involved in that project.

Finding a remedy for a risk in not necessary difficult. You just have to find a remedy, not solve the problem. Finding a remedy is important, so you can assign the person or department responsible to take care of it. And once you have assigned a responsibility to a particular risk, then you do not have a risk anymore, you have an assumption. Hence, you have just converted a risk to an assumption!

A good example will be a social setting, such as the local community softball team. You may be the coach, treasurer, administrator, or the player, the scenario is pretty much the same. Take uniforms, for instance. Let's say the uniforms are old and must be replaced. And you are selected to help replace those uniforms. Well, your project then is the "Uniform Replacement". Regardless of what the common consensus is in the team, the old uniforms are not your problem, in fact they are assumptions.

You must act on Risk Equalization as soon as you take command. Quickly assign a responsibility for the old uniform, and they will be off your hands. In fact, if you do not act right away, I guarantee you that those old uniforms will become a risk, and you will be left to handle it.

This is exactly how it is in corporate Project Management. Project Managers that do not pay attention to Risk Equalization are left with a lot more loose ends to take care of. But it does not stop there, you must officially have a list of assumptions and risks, and document it.

First, you must identify *all* risks, without documenting it. For example, the disposal of the old uniforms will be one of the risks. Another common risk may be the lack of suppliers in your price range to purchase the uniforms from. Or even the deadline allocated to you.

Second, study all the risks, to see which ones you can assign to other people.

Third, delegate a risk value to the risk, one being a low risk, and five being a critical risk. This is an important delegation, as it will keep everyone abreast of the aggregate view of the risk game.

Fourth, make an official list of the assumptions and all the risks.

For example:

ASSUMPTIONS:

- Maintenance committee will dispose off all the old uniforms

RISKS:

- Lack of suppliers in price range—Value 4

- Deadline January 3, 2002 may be too short—Value 3

- Number of players may increase for the 2003 season—Value 2

- Color Blue may have to added to the uniforms to give it a more patriotic look—Value 2

You will always have a few risks that are left over. It is not the objective of Risk Equalization to convert all the risk to assumption, or be unfair to the other members of the community. You are simply managing the situation, and are being just to the organization, in placing the right components where they belong.

Let me offer a word of caution here. If you are dealing with an outside entity, such as a social club or an organization, be careful in performing Risk Equalization, lest you will estrange yourself. There are two core reasons for this, Discounting Risk and Receiving Risk.

DISCOUNTING RISK

Consider the sensitivity of your client, in this case, the organization that you are serving. For example, what kind of an importance is the organization delegating to the risk? Is it a huge burden on them? Is it important for them to have someone with your capability take care of it?

You are discounting a risk every time you convert it to an assumption, or creating an environment, where you are designating the risk a lower risk level. Hence, if you delegate a value of 2 to a risk, which the organization takes very seriously, you may be identified as someone who does not take his/her job very seriously.

Or, as in the case above, your risk conversion may be seen as *passing the buck*. Evaluate your risks carefully, and if your analysis reveals that the risk discounts will cause ill will, then you may consider not performing Risk Equalization, or keeping it to a minimum.

In fact, in my other books and articles, I have even gone as far as to suggest making an effort in identifying two kinds of risks, Touchable Risks and Untouchable Risks. Let this list thrive in a concealed mood of clandestine. Convert the Touchable Risks, but study the Untouchable Risks till you are very comfortable with the organization, then tackle them in a careful and politically astute way.

RECEIVING RISK

How about the person, who will be inheriting the risk, or the now assumption? As you can imagine, the receiving party will never be too thrilled to receive the risk. The only way to perform this conversion is to test out multiple receiving parties. Have more then one person in mind. Study these people, as if you are a predator, and you are tracking your prey.

Then move in for the kill. Identify the final receiver and assign.

Wait for a few days, and see what happens. Chances are that if you have done your homework, and gathered your intelligence, you will have no problems. If you do, go back to the original receiver, and recruit that person's help in locating your next target. I assure you that you will have a motivated helper.

If all else fails, depending on your prominence with the organization, either you have to bite the bullet, or be a manager, and just make the decision, as to who will get the conversion. Risk Equalizer is a very innovative tool, and may be a bit uncomfortable to use, if you do not posses the appropriate people skills. Try anyway, as the objective here is not just to look good, but also to serve others, efficiently and effectively.

Review of Family and Friends

I suppose this section could really have fit anywhere, but given the exposure you already have received on Life Wizard's Perfect Life Management, I believe you are ready to take on a little change of pace. I will risk my faith in you by giving this gem of an interactive chapter I call, Review and Appraisal Based on Family-Friends Attributes, or RABOFA.

We endure labels from people we know, even some people we don't know. We are constantly judged, reviewed, and evaluated. The resulting labels we apply to people become a baseline for our interaction with them. It is unfortunate, but these labels become a permanent part of the people, and even more disturbing, it becomes part of their psyche. The disquieting outcome resulting from this is that we deal with our family and friends, based on the review that someone else has done on him or her, or more correctly, *to them*.

I believe that you should do your own review. And depending on your relationship with the subject, you will guide them in the direction, which will make them close to a Life Wizard. You may have a slight reluctance to do this, but do not be troubled, read RABOFA, and you will agree that this is the best way.

RABOFA

Before we begin to embark on this exciting interactive chapter…Interactive of sorts, since eventually you will be using this information to probe and help people. Thus before we begin, allow me to give you an interesting insight in RABOFA.

RABOFA was actually once RABOHA. RABOHA stands for Review and Appraisal Based on Human Attributes. Actually it should stand for Review and Appraisal Based on Employee Attributes, but then I would have to call it RABOEA, and frankly I liked RABOHA better. RABOHA is the predecessor to RABOFA.

RABOHA was created to help the manager conduct the review in the employee's environment. Basically, the manager observes the employee's behavior, and then takes action to give kudos, or *change* the employee's behavior. Here is the tale of RABOHA.

Few years ago, I was part of an exciting project in a desert town in West Texas. During this project, I had the good fortune to be involved with the employees of the project, outside the work environment. I started my study at that time, and five years later I had RABOHA. I do recognize that my methods were unique, but it is important for me to share the events leading to RABOHA, so you can get a better understanding of it.

I made some interesting observations. I noticed that although most of the employees had a certain professional disposition during work hours, they displayed similar characteristics during the off-work hours. For example, if John was characteristically cheery during the work hours, then he would have a parallel cheery temperament during the off-work hours. Similarly, if Jane had a sulky attitude during the work hours, then she would maintain most of the same attitude during the off-work hours.

At this point, I was trying to conceptualize about two things. If the employees appeared to be happy, were they really happy? And more importantly, if they were happy, then did they work better? My aim was to seek the answers to those basic human emotions, to determine how their moods affect their performance, and how they could be organized for better production to benefit all.

Here is my main point. The idea was not to change the mood of the employee, but to work with the current temperament that they possessed. For example, if John, as a happy employee, performed better, then we have to advise and guide Jane to bring her to the same level of John. I had to essentially create a methodology, which will conduct reviews *and* make specific recommendations, to increase the overall production, and improve the quality of interaction with other employees.

Hence, after 60 more months of gathering data and observing humans in industries like Aviation, Biologics, Finance, Retail, and Education, I had RABOHA. And now we have RABOFA. Based on the same principals of RABOHA, but a very uncomplicated review process, where the Life Wizard can select the "Attributes" relating to a particular person, then merely going to the corresponding "Action Paragraph" and applying that recommendation to that person.

Our end result of this section will be to formulate a professional report. We will do this by taking all the Attributes and their matching Action Paragraphs, and putting it together, just like a professional manager to form the Attribute Report. And of course, based on your needs, you can either share it with that person, or keep it a secret, and help them clandestinely. Whatever you decide, the review system is designed to be shared with the person being reviewed.

Of course we have to remember that no project is successful without a sense of integrity and social responsibility. And you will certainly be helping the people you review. But in order for RABOFA to be effective, you have to confront and cooperate with the selfish side of it. Here is why:

It does not matter what year you are reading this book in, maybe it is 2002, or 2202 if you look back just ten years, you will realize how much the times have changed. Especially in the case of being bombarded by opinions and attitudes. We watch TV (substitute the latest invention here!), listen to radios, watch more TV, read books, watch even more TV, well you get the point. Whether you like it on not, your combined opinion are a result of a collection of opinions. And opinions form outlook, outlook influences your actions, and your actions affect the core of the quality of your life.

Yes, we can control what goes in our heads. We can switch books, change channels, and be alert of our thoughts. But we tend to fail to notice a major source of the thought bombardment. These come from the people we interact with everyday. These are our friends, our family, and our co-workers. We are influenced by the great encouragement and positive enforcement that we get from them, as well as the negative junk that we must endure from our everyday partners in life.

Hence, the second purpose of RABOFA. It will be great to help and conform the people you deal with to be more positive toward you, and have a great quality of life, but you must be aware of who they are, and most importantly, what they are. And you must take the appropriate action to ensure that only the most positive and the most productive bunch influence your life.

The RABOFA worksheet is quite unambiguous, and easy to follow. Simply read the attribute, and check "Yes" or "No". If you feel the need to write a comment, or a note, for a future recollection, write it in the remark section. As you read and go further in this section, you might want to create your own attribute, based on your present environment, and consequently your own customized report on your friends, family, and anybody you feel influences your state of mind.

And finally, remember that the review is not designed to dig out the person's attitude or actions toward you, but in general the way the person conducts work, interpersonal relationship, and everyday life. Thus, giving you a detailed indication of the person's workings, this will help you determine on a long-term strategy in how you will deal with this person.

As you interact with this section of the book, remember these operational requirements:

1. The purpose of the Life Wizard is to utilize the methodology developed for the often-unforgiving business world, in the personal world. Hence the very austere appearance subject of the review worksheet. In reality, the quintessential benefits of the review and the results are there.

2. Do not let the repetition of the word "person" throw you off. The mundane word "person" represents a friend, a family member, or a co-worker. This is necessary to slightly distance yourself with this individual that you are reviewing, in order to grant you more objectivity.

3. Change your state of mind right now. Take a few seconds, close your eyes, and imagine yourself as a wise old person, about to embark on a journey to help all those who will cross your path. You are about to be a sagacious leader, in a position of helping and guiding a lot of people.

4. I have used the terms, "friends", "family members", and "co-workers" interchangeably to avoid the boredom of equivalent labeling. Use whichever applies, and is most appropriate in your particular setting.

5. You will notice that the phrase "your needs" is used liberally. If "your needs" echoes as too egotistical for your taste, feel free to replace it with whatever phrase that has a comfortable resonance for you, such as "your requirements".

6. It is assumed that you will be using these individuals in one of the methodology presented in Life Wizardry, for Perfect Life Management.

WARNING:

Before you enter the next section, let me fairly warn you that if you are not comfortable with your own virtues, you will be inclined to disseminate empty advice, and not actually help the people. Your main objective will be that of a taker, and not a giver. And you will compromise the two main objectives of this very important piece of Life Wizardry, which are, to have a reasonable control in how others affect your state of mind, and your facility to help others rise to your level.

If you feel that you are not ready to proceed, you may skip to the following chapters, and then come back to this section, when you feel comfortable.

If you are ready, then let us begin:

1. Attribute—OFFERS YOU NEW IDEAS:

Yes:

Remarks:

No:

Remarks:

Let the person see the big picture. Sometimes the person may see a *better* or *quicker* way of doing things. However, in the big picture, with the new idea introduced, all the components may not work together as well. Keep a very open mind, when the person suggests an idea; that is, consider the possibility of changing a *certain* way of doing things.

Transcend the experience barrier, if the person is a young child, or a new person in your life. Treat them as true team members in your project, or whatever goal or objective you are working toward.

2. Attribute—FUNCTIONS INDEPENDTLY:

Yes:

Remarks:

No:

Remarks:

The person must see the objectives clearly, so as not to trample on the end results. If you are using this person in your project, or if he/she is a potential manipulator of the outcome somehow, then very carefully keep tabs on the personal goals articulated by the person; it must be directly aligned, in terms of values and principles, as yours.

Evaluate the person's given tasks. Ensure that those tasks are met reasonably by the person, and are not compromised by the person's independent actions.

3. Attribute—LACKS INITIATIVE:

Yes:

Remarks:

No:

Remarks:

Let the person feel free to suggest new ideas and take action on them, as the present way may not be the best fit in the process. The person actually may possess some unique qualities, which can be beneficial to you. Introduce the person to key players in your family, or friend circle, so that they may influence the person.

For example, if you meet a new friend, introduce this person to your family. Or if dealing with a family member, introduce this person to your outside friends and co-workers. When asked for advice, delay in giving one, and let the person come up with the solution.

4. Attribute—NOT WILLING TO TAKE RISKS:

Yes:

Remarks:

No:

Remarks:

Give the person an opportunity to work on a small project, where the end result does not constitute a great degree of significance. Let the person be aware that wrong or inappropriate decisions will be permissible. Downplay the importance of the friend or family member this person may be about to meet.

Stress your personal mission, and how certain decisions will have to be made to accomplish these objectives. When a change is noticed in the person's behavior, make sure proper reward is given; even if it is in the form of encouraging words.

5. Attribute—VERY PRODUCTIVE:

Yes:

Remarks:

No:

Remarks:

The person must give precedence to the tasks that have priority. That is, the person has to be productive on the tasks that's summoning for prioritization, in line with your goals. Reorganize and overhaul the requirements of the project this person is assigned to, if needed, but ensure that the person keeps the edge on being productive. At the same time the person must concentrate on the business that matters most. Do not allow the person to work in isolation, let the whole family share in the richness of productivity.

6. Attribute—USES TIME EFFICIENTLY AND EFFECTIVELY:

Yes:

Remarks:

No:

Remarks:

Reevaluate the person's schedule carefully. Include all the variables, such as school, work, playtime, and downtime. Appraise and estimate the major tasks the person has completed in the past two to four weeks. You have to ensure that the efficiency that is being modeled is actually work that deserves the time and attention that the person has been giving it. Give the person a particularly difficult task, or go to this person with a personal problem, and thoughtfully analyze the time spent on it. This will give you a good idea of the person's true potential.

7. Attribute—NOT ORGANIZED IN WORK:

Yes:

Remarks:

No:

Remarks:

Start from the basics. For example, if the subject is your child, then have him/her clean the work area of all loose papers and out of date personal effects, such as, old birthday invitations and such.

Next, ensure that the person is using all the computer resources in an optimal basis. If this person does not have a computer, try and acquire this resource for the person. If the person does not have a high-tech forte, train the person. If you do not have a high-tech forte, then get some training.

Reduce paper by storing and backing up everything that can be stored electronically. Carefully keep track of the person's path of efficiency on a daily basis, that is, see in what order the person accomplishes the tasks on an hour-to-hour basis.

8. Attribute—PROCRASTINATES:

Yes:

Remarks:

No:

Remarks:

Help the person prioritize the day. The person must spend the first ten minutes of the day making a list of things to be done arranged in order of importance. Ensure that the person has a precise deadline for all the tasks. When these deadlines are met, reward the person. Make him/her aware that an effort is being made to overcome the procrastination.

9. Attribute—HAS DIFFICULT PRIORITIZING:

Yes:

Remarks:

No:

Remarks:

The person must work out of a deadline-based system. Keep all the tasks on the list in view at all times, and ensure that the person does not pick the tasks that are based on interest, or what the person feels is of particular importance for whatever reason. Help the person here identify which tasks are applicable to your goals and objectives. He/she must keep in touch with other members of the team, to constantly remind oneself that the objectives and priorities must be aligned across teams.

10. Attribute—UNDERSTANDS YOUR NEEDS:

Yes:

Remarks:

No:

Remarks:

Use the person's understanding of your needs. If your needs are too ambiguous, in relation to this person, then revise and redefine your needs. He/she must be given a leadership role in your group to further expand the understanding to the rest of your friends and family, to serve as a role model to others.

Develop a secret training program based on these new findings. Use your imagination unreservedly to train the people around you to respond to your needs. Assign this person to play a key role in designing this new course of action that suite your needs.

11. Attribute—GOOD DISPOSITION TOWARD YOU:

Yes:

Remarks:

No:

Remarks:

Use the person's disposition toward you to further enhance the total satisfaction package. Identify what motivated the person and disseminate this intelligence among other persons. Once again, use the secret training program based on these new findings. Study the motivation of this person carefully, and try to replicate the same feelings in other members of your family and friends.

12. Attribute—PROMPTLY RESPONDS TO YOU:

Yes:

Remarks:

No:

Remarks:

Ensure that the person is pragmatic and honest toward your expectations. Monitor the person's zeal to satisfy you, and ensure it does not take precedence over the person's ability to provide realistic service to others.

Have your current schedule always available to the person. Have appropriate rewards ready for the person for meeting your needs, and even for providing service to others. Grant this person enough authority to carry out tactical decisions on your behalf.

13. Attribute—UNCLEAR ON YOUR NEEDS:

Yes:

Remarks:

No:

Remarks:

Quiz this person on your needs and requirements. Keep a tab on the depth of ambiguousness and vagueness this person displays. Document the level of understanding that the person has of the current needs. If the results are unsatisfactory, schedule yourself to spend some time with this person to reacquaint him/her with your needs. If all fails, remove this person from any position that might affect you adversely.

14. Attribute—UNRESPONSIVE TO YOU:

Yes:

Remarks:

No:

Remarks:

If this person displays the attribute of being unclear on your needs, follow the advice below. However, if the person is truly unresponsive to you, and displays antagonism toward you, remove this person form your daily activities.

If he/she is a family member, obviously a little bit more effort is needed in your part to enlighten him/her to your requirements. As your needs are crucial to you, have a specific deadline to correct this problem. Be prepared to remove this person from your life's daily activities.

15. Attribute—INTERACTS EFFECTIVELY WITH YOUR FRIENDS AND FAMILY:

Yes:

Remarks:

No:

Remarks:

Let this person work on many different tasks. If this person is a family member, then let him/her interact and constantly communicate with your friends and co-workers. Use this person as a catalyst to improve communication in your whole organization. Ensure that this person is clear on your goals, as this person's vision and value will likely transfer to other persons.

16. Attribute—PROVIDES ACCURATE INFORMATION:

Yes:

Remarks:

No:

Remarks:

Occasionally double check the accuracy of this person, do not assume that the information will always be accurate. Besides accuracy, verify that all the important material is included in the information he/she is providing you.

If all works out fine, push this person a little. Encourage this person more and engage him/her in more conversations. Have this person talk to all your friends and family members at length, so that his/her reporting is more comprehensive.

17. Attribute—COMMUNICATES WELL:

Yes:

Remarks:

No:

Remarks:

Having a loud voice, or talking a lot does not qualify this person as a good communicator. Monitor the reaction of your other friends and family members, when this person is speaking.

If your understanding is correct about this person being a good communicator, then have this person attend a lot of your meetings and other gatherings that include key leaders from the organization and families. Ensure that this person has all the proper information and the knowledge to interact in this capacity.

If this person is a professional in the technical field, such as a computer consultant, or a programmer, instruct this person to avert from using too much technical jargon. Coach this person to speak on your behalf.

18. Attribute—POOR LISTENER:

Yes:

Remarks:

No:

Remarks:

Observe the person during a conversation for signs of acknowledgement. If the person indicates that the information is not being adequately absorbed, ask occasional questions. Ask questions constantly, if a reasonable answer is not given, confront the person.

Help the person along by handing over books and other training material to improve their listening skills. Depending on your comfort level with this person, explain to the person that his/her quality of relationship to you may depend in the person being more attentive.

19. Attribute—DOES NOT HAVE A PRESENTABLE APPEAR-
ANCE:

Yes:

Remarks:

No:

Remarks:

Determine what makes this person not have a presentable appear-ance. Focus on the person's attitude, demeanor, body language, and clothes. Look for evidence of an affectation, which may have gone awry, such as a neglected beard, or a bizarre hairstyle. Inform the per-son about your dress code.

If you do not have a dress code, then prepare one. Do not single one person out. Make sure an even standard is observed. If all fails, do not expose this person in a group, where a dress code faux pas may cause you embarrassment, or a loss of social standing points. It is assumed that you know better, but do not, under any circumstances, hurt this person's feeling, while executing the remedy for this review result.

20. Attribute—UNABLE TO EXPRESS IDEAS:

Yes:

Remarks:

No:

Remarks:

This person should study your friends or family members, before expressing his/her ideas. Assist the person in preparing detailed outlines, for social conversations and other similar situations. Offer guidance relating to the use of appropriate rhetoric.

Instruct the person to be as straightforward and direct as possible. Knowledge transfer is important. If this person continues to have problems with expressing ideas, reposition the person to a different role in your life.

21. Attribute—WORKS WELL IN YOUR GROUP:

Yes:

Remarks:

No:

Remarks:

Assign this person a mediator's role during your conflicts. Let the person communicate candidly with your friends and family members. Remind the person to be impartial and fair in these meetings. Suggest to your friends or family how well they work together, when this person is present. Encourage other divisions of the company you keep to apply the person's skill for their benefit.

22. Attribute—WORKS TOWARD YOUR GOALS:

Yes:

Remarks:

No:

Remarks:

Assign this person a mediator's role during any conflict that you may experience in your life. Use this person in plans for your long-term goals. Ensure that the goals are strategic in nature, as well as tactical.

Let the essence of goal setting carry through in your environment. It should touch all of your friends and family, in an abstract basis.

Scrutinize the goals to ensure that they are distinct and obtainable Periodically review the goals to ensure that they are in-line with the overall goals and vision of your future. Ask for input, when there are organizational changes made that affect yours or your family's previous goals.

23. Attribute—ABLE TO RESOLVE INTERPERSONAL DIS-
CORD:

Yes:

Remarks:

No:

Remarks:

Have this person remain objective and unbiased at all times. Examine the motives behind the person's disposition for the interpersonal
skills. Ensure that the ultimate intent and motive for this social grace is
not personal in nature, but also conforms to your ultimate needs. Have
the person mingle and blend in different groups. Allow the person to
play a key role in all your gatherings.

24. Attribute—FINDS FAULTS IN YOUR GROUP MEMBERS:

Yes:

Remarks:

No:

Remarks:

Help the person understand that all your friends and family members, as well as some co-workers care about you, and are working to accomplish the same objectives and goals.

Observe the person for signs of frustration, when dealing with other persons. If not of the immediate family, examine the background of the person carefully, to check for any signs of violence at home, or in the work environment in the past.

If the person's temperament varies from finding faults to outright verbal criticism, then consider suggesting to this person some sensitivity training, formal training or informally conducted by you. If all fails, remove the person from your life.

25. Attribute—DOES NOT SHARE INFORMATION:

Yes:

Remarks:

No:

Remarks:

Occasionally interrogate the person to determine what type of information he/she has been exposed to. If the information is not too personal in nature, inquire whether the person shared the ideas with all the mutual contacts. The notion here is to make the person perceive and understand that it is mutually advantageous to exchange vital information. Illustrate to the person the undeviating correlation between the success of the friends and family, and the success of the person.

26. Attribute—ADAPTS TO CHANGES:

Yes:

Remarks:

No:

Remarks:

Encourage the person by elucidating the value of being able to change with the environment. Demonstrate the contribution the person is making by being able to change. Further encourage the person to be proactive in the change.

Although being adaptive is commendable, ensure that the person does not just move forward, without any regard to the satisfactory fulfillment of his/her services to you. Verify that tasks handed over to the person are fully completed.

27. Attribute—OPEN TO NEW IDEAS:

Yes:

Remarks:

No:

Remarks:

This person needs all the support you can give, as long as the ideas are received, and ultimately acted upon for your and your family's benefit. Monitor the ideas being fed into this person to ensure that they are not detrimental to your overall goals.

Help the person generate new ideas, instead of just acting upon new ideas being furnished. Also, assist the person in being open to all ideas, not just the ones that meet certain person-defined guidelines.

28. Attribute—PROACTIVE:

Yes:

Remarks:

No:

Remarks:

Keep track of this person for at least a few weeks to shadow the effects of the actions taken. Look for scenarios to catch potential problems.

Lend a hand to the person to have contingency plans handy, in case of failure of the original plan. Being proactive has its hazards; a lot more action items are created, and ultimately acted upon.

Entrust this person with tasks that deal with issues that are stagnant for you, especially those issues that have suffered from dullness and inaction in the past.

Delegate more responsibility to this person; quickly raise him/her to bequeath more power and authority in your life, so the person can make the proactive characteristic work more practically and efficiently.

29. Attribute—DOES NOT ADAPT WITHOUT CONTROL:

Yes:

Remarks:

No:

Remarks:

Ask the person to take ownership of the problem often. Monitor how much time you spent on this person dealing with his/her problems. Inform the person that answerability and responsibility will be of significance.

Present the person with substantially difficult tasks, and do not make yourself available that often, for a few weeks. Notice signs of confidence evolving in the person. Build confidence by conferring with the person's immediate family and friends to employ similar means of confidence building techniques.

30. Attribute—UNWILLING TO TAKE ON VARYING CHAL-
LENGES:

Yes:

Remarks:

No:

Remarks:

Inform the person on the importance of the tasks by giving evidence of the importance of the challenges in the scheme of things in life. Make challenges more engaging to the person. Probe in to the reason behind the apprehensiveness of the person.

Structure the task to be a little easier, or respite it down to a manageable size. Acquaint the person, in a non-threatening manner, with the responsibilities and accountability of his/her challenge. Make evident to the person how this challenge will ultimately affect the person's life.

31. Attribute—TREATS OTHERS FAIRLY:

Yes:

Remarks:

No:

Remarks:

Examine this person's style to make sure that it is indeed fair, and just does not appear to be so. At times, when the Life Managers are biased toward the popular persons, the perception can be a little skewed.

Quiz the person on the issues at stake. Ensure that the person is very clear on the different issues and their priorities that you and your family and friends are facing.

Furnish more responsibilities to this person, and notice if his/her manners and attitudes change. Determine the peak of diminishing proficiency for this person.

See how far he/she can be pushed, as far as a favorable attitude toward you and your family, before evidence of exhaustion is experienced. If this person is genuinely a fair person, you will be able to gauge the depth of his/her fairness.

32. Attribute—HAS CLARITY IN VISION AND FOCUS:

Yes:

Remarks:

No:

Remarks:

Take this person's ideas and sculpture it to fit your needs. When the person suggests an idea, assist the person in removing everyday obstacles. Refine and clarify the vision to meet your goals and objectives. Seek the person's input in all significant affairs. Promote this person in your scheme of things, where more strategic initiative is needed.

33. Attribute—JUDGEMENT IS SOMETIMES BIASED:

Yes:

Remarks:

No:

Remarks:

Study and recognize the reason behind the bias. If it is related to quality, performance, or other legitimate reason, work with the person to refine the methods. Otherwise clarify the persons role in your environment to reflect the seriousness of this shortcoming. Ensure that all your values are in order, as well. Check all the other members of this person's family and close associates to ensure that their judgment and focus is acceptable to your standards.

34. Attribute—DOES NOT CHALLENGE DIFFICULT ISSUES:

Yes:

Remarks:

No:

Remarks:

Ask the person to seek your help in making key decisions, with respect to difficult issues, regardless of the complexity. Slowly build the person's confidence to make the decisions independently. If an issue arises, stay out of the issue as much as possible. Offer your help to the person only as a last resort. Once a difficult issue is handled, support the decision attained by the person.

35. Attribute—WILLING TO GAIN KNOWLEDGE:

Yes:

Remarks:

No:

Remarks:

Ensure that the person is acquiring knowledge, which can be directly used for your mutual benefit. Ask the person to make a list of skills, which might need improvement. Make time available for him/her. Draw up a long-term plan with the person. Give your relationship some direction, as to how it will ultimately benefit the completeness of your life. Impress upon the person the personal benefits to be gained by advancing oneself in knowledge.

36. Attribute—CONSCIENTIOUS AND ETHICAL:

Yes:

Remarks:

No:

Remarks:

Assist and encourage this person in transmitting these qualities to as many people as possible, especially those people in your realm of existence.

Monitor the stability of these merits, and if found to be consistent, move the person around within different groups in your family, or social circle.

Nourish this belief system even further by rewarding this person often. For example, take this person out to lunch or a show.

Seek this person's advice before implementing new policies and procedures in your life. Especially ones that promise to bring major change. Acquire this person's assistance in making decisions in issues dealing with ethical problems.

37. Attribute—HAS TROUBLE WITH TIME MANAGEMENT:

Yes:

Remarks:

No:

Remarks:

Keep a detailed log of tasks performed by this person. Include in the log any deviation from the accepted arrival time at gatherings and other occasions.

Verify whether the person is simply taking too much on, or is truly having trouble managing time. In the former case, assist the person in delegating authority.

If needed, help the person out by running some errands. If the person is constantly underestimating the time for task completion, investigate the reasons behind it.

Ensure that the person is getting accurate information from the regular sources, and there is nobody is trying to social sabotage him/her.

38. Attribute—GETS INVOLVED WITH CHATTER AND GOS-
SIP:

Yes:

Remarks:

No:

Remarks:

Notice carefully how much time productiveness is being wasted by these undesirable qualities. Observe, but leave the person alone, if the affect on you is inconsequential.

However, if these habits prove to be a problem, explain to this person the consequences of being sidetracked and time wastage. Nothing brings the moral down in persons then hearing some worthless and futile gossip.

Clarify and control any misinformation already spread. However, be realistic in implementing any plans to remedy this situation.

If the gossip is about you, or involves you in any way, don't waste any time in establishing distance between you and this person.

39. Attribute—EXHIBITS NEGATIVE THOUGHTS:

Yes:

Remarks:

No:

Remarks:

This is the last on the list, because it is the most important. If any-thing can bring down your dreams and goals, it is negative thinking. Unfortunately, negative thinking is very contagious. It will provide you with doubt, hesitation, uncertainty, and indecision. The easy thing would be to stay away from this person at all cost. However, due to the seriousness of the subject, you must gently steer this person in the right direction to get the true glimpse of life, which makes it worth the mag-nificent journey it is.

If your action for this attribute is hindered by your own deficiencies in positive thinking, I encourage you to look up authors like Napoleon Hill and Norman Vincent Peale, who have graced humanity in this century. In fact, there are many individuals from our present time who can make a gigantic difference in your life. Authors and speakers such as Wayne Dyer, Deepak Chopra, and Anthony Robbins are my favorites. I have personally turned my life around with the help of these people. As a matter of fact, I would like to go as far as to soundly propose to you that you pick up something from the above authors.

The reason you have felt such assertion and pronouncement from me to access the brilliant minds of these people, is not just what you learn about the unqualified truth about positive thinking, but about what is possible. And as you stand in your present timeline, let me tell you now unequivocally that what is possible is explicitly beyond your comprehension. And I say this not because I believe that you are incapable of imagination, I say this because of humanity's incapability of deciphering the infinite number of variables that are constantly being thrown at us in our universe.

INCLINATIONS FOR THE REVIEW

Can you describe what happened in the last 40 pages or so? It was a melange of practicing to be wickedly selfish, compassionately selfless, and thoughtfully introspective. You saw your friends, family, and co-workers, as a manager would see his/her people, in a cold and evaluative gaze. At the same time, if you so feel inclined, you can experience a very clean vision of how to draw them out of mediocrity, and bring out the sharp and focused outlook of objective reasoning and effective productively.

But therein lies the problem, doesn't it? Do you have the relationship comfort or the leadership inclination to perform the necessary analysis, and take the subsequent actions? Perhaps you should take this review process as a separate mission. Determine what your requirements are, and establish what steps you are willing to take to achieve your objectives.

The first step is to honestly ask yourself, "How many of the review attribute actions do you have the ability to perform?" If your answer is less then you like, that is quite okay. Just tackle a few of the review attribute actions at a time. If you do not wish to take any action, then that is quite okay as well. Perform those review attribute actions, which will give you an insight in the people you engage with frequently. Perhaps that will be a good starting point for a better tomorrow.

Walking the Critical Path

If you have been so inclined as to put your daily activities in the category of a project, you will see different opportunities for their executions. You may imagine *driving* to the library as a drive, or you may see it as a *stopover* before the grocery store, or you may even see it just as a quick drop-off point for the books. The task of going to the library fits in some sequence of events.

The Critical Path Method is a Project Management technique, which allows you to see the sequence of events of all the tasks, and the time required. With Critical Path Method, you can also chart the earliest finish, earliest start, latest finish, and latest start estimates, so you can see the *slack* in each of these tasks. The idea here is to see the *dependencies* of each of these tasks.

Once you are aware of the slack in your program, you can arrange and rearrange the tasks to optimize your time. And once you get a good picture of the tasks, you can then dive in the sub-tasks to guarantee a good Critical Path, and assure the successful completion of your project, which in this case is the sum total of your daily activities.

At this time let me introduce you to Milestones. Milestones are merely noteworthy events in your project. And as the name implies, Milestones are just that. It does not have a beginning or an end; Ipso facto, it does not have duration. Hence, you may define Milestones as *tasks with duration of zero.*

I use Milestones as a checkpoint for the completion of a major phase. For example, in my Project 01-13-02, which is the sum of all activities that I will be conducting on Sunday, January 13, 2002, I have arranged my tasks, subtasks, and Milestones as follows:

TASK—SUBTASKS—MILESTONES LIST

1. Phase I—Morning

    1.1. Task 1—Library

        1.1.1. Drop off books

        1.1.2. Browse new DVD section

        1.1.3. Browse section on Hemingway

        1.1.4. Browse new audio books

            1.1.4.1. Check out selected audio books

    1.2. Task 2—Bank branch

        1.2.1. Draw $100 for day expenses

        1.2.2. Close out safety deposit box

Completion of Phase I—MILESTONE

2. Phase II—Afternoon

    2.1. Task 3—Gym

        2.1.1. Indoor track run

            2.1.1.1. 2 miles

        2.1.2. Sit-up machine

            2.1.2.1. 3 sets

                2.1.2.1.1. 20 reps

        2.1.3. Lat Pull-down machine

            2.1.3.1. 3 sets

                2.1.3.1.1. 20 reps

    2.2. Task 4—Grocery store

2.2.1. Food

    2.2.1.1. Croissants

    2.2.1.2. Margarine

    2.2.1.3. Cereal

    2.2.1.4. Milk

2.2.2. Non food

    2.2.2.1. Aluminum foil

    2.2.2.2. Water filter

Completion of Phase II—MILESTONE

3. Phase III—Late afternoon

    3.1. Task 5—Home stopover

        3.1.1. Drop off supplies

        3.1.2. Lunch

    3.2. Task 6—Lake walk

        3.2.1. Walk around lake with Salma (wife)

        3.2.2. Chase after ducks

    3.3. Task 7—Attend movie

        3.3.1. Movie theater (movie to be decided)

Completion of Phase III—MILESTONE

Believe it or not, this is a very accurate task list for me on a typical Sunday. If I did not follow all my Life Wizardry, Perfect Life Management techniques, I would not be able to do even half of these tasks. Notice that we do not have a schedule allocated to this yet, or for that matter, a budget, a resource list, or even a breakdown structure. This all comes later, at this point, we are concerned with the flow of the tasks, and how they may interrelate to each other.

I tend to follow a schedule similar to this next Sunday. And I followed one last week. However, the tasks and the schedule differ from week to week. The tasks are similar, not exact. So the project is never the same, if it were, then it would not be a project any more, it would be a process.

As you can see from the task list that we can go to some substantial details for each of the task; you may choose not to. In fact, I will not go in the details, or the sub-tasks, in the Critical Path. But I find it very accommodating to list out the sub-tasks to help me with the widespread view of the whole project.

In construction of the Critical Path Method we will use the main tasks only. If you feel up to it, and more adventurous, feel free to use the sub-tasks also, but it will take you a long time.

To start the Critical Path Method, break down the project into tasks. Assign an abstract schedule to each task. For example, instead of saying 10:AM to 12:PM for the library task, assign it a conceptual timeline, for instance, two hours. Include the driving times.

Line up the tasks. Similar to what we did in the previous page. However, if you are not using the sub-tasks, you may employ a different visual diagram. For example, draw it out in a linear fashion, such as:

Library (2hrs) - Bank (45 min) - Gym (1.5 hrs) - Grocery (1 hr) - Home (1.5 hrs) - Walk (30 min) - Movie (2.5 hrs)

Study the sequence very carefully. Does it make sense? For example, in this case, you may consider the logistics of driving to the several locations. From my home in the suburbs in Illinois, I can go straight on Main Street, and approach the Township Library. Then logistically it would make sense if I went to the bank, as it is right next to the library. Once there, it would make further sense to go grocery shopping.

However, in my case, as I do not want to carry the food in my car, I decided to go to the gym, and then visit the grocery store. You get the idea, use logic, use rationale, and any specialized information you have.

Once you have surely decided on the sequence, divide the tasks into two groups, Most Optimistic (MO) finish estimate, and Most Pessimistic (MP) finish estimate, and label the tasks (without any values) to set the whole thing up for the Critical Path Method:

Library (2 hrs) (MP) (MO) - Bank (45 min) (MO) (MP) - Gym (1.5 hrs) (MO) (MP) - Grocery (1 hr) (MO) (MP) - Home (1.5 hrs) (MO) (MP) - Walk (30 min) (MO) (MP) - Movie (2.5 hrs) (MO) (MP)

This is the raw material for the Critical Path Method.

Now assign the most optimistic finish estimate, and most pessimistic finish estimate values. For example, from experience I know that once we get to the library, sometimes my wife vanishes in Psychology books, or I get spell bound by Emerson, or Thoreau, or some other genius of our time. And the time can be two hours, or more.

Of course, sometimes the time can be estimated with some accuracy. For instance, I know the little branch of the bank we go to on a Sunday afternoon is never busy, and it may not take more then one hour, but at least that to finish our business.

Or in the case of the walk, if I get bored of the ducks and not want to antagonize them, I may want to quit in 15 minutes.

In any case, the time assignment should have the following expression:

Library (2hrs) (MO 1.5 hrs) (MP 2.5 hrs) - Bank (45 min) (MO 45 min) (MP 1 hr) - Gym (1.5 hrs) (MO 1 hr) (MP 2.5 hrs) - Grocery (1 hr) (MO 30 min) (MP 2 hrs) - Home (1.5 hrs) (MO 1.5 hrs) (MP 2.5 hrs) - Walk (30 min) (MO 15 min) (MP 30 min) - Movie (2.5 hrs) (MO 2 hrs) (MP 3 hrs)

Hint: Lay the above equation down on paper as liner as the length of the paper permits.

The next step is to acquire a few diverse angles to this. As the most likely time, we had designated 9.75 hours (9 hrs and 45 minutes). But based on the MO values, we can complete the day in 7.5 hours (7hrs and 30 minutes), and based on the MP values, we could complete the day in 14 hours.

That is, if everything goes according to plan, we could be back home sitting next to the fireplace in less then eight hours, and if nothing goes according to the plan, then we could get home at midnight!

Do you see the value in Critical Path? Although it seems like common sense, it makes a lot more sense, when we give it clarity on paper.

We are not finished yet. We can conduct a more precise analysis by applying the slack time. The slack time default value of any task is zero. It will be more realistic to assume that the whole day will be a combination of the Most Optimistic and the Most Pessimistic time estimates. At this conjecture, we can use the slack times.

For example, in the library example, the MO value is 2, and the MP value is 2.5, hence the slack time is the result of the subtraction of the two values:

2.5 hrs - 1.5 hrs = .5 hrs Or 30 minutes

Hence, if we show up at the library at 10:00 AM, and we get out of there at 11:30 AM (using the 30 minutes slack time), we can actually start our second task early. Also, we know the latest time we will leave the library by using slack time, which is 12:30 PM. Slack time is the total time that tasks can be late without upsetting the conclusion time of the day.

When you continue this logic in relation to all the tasks, you will notice that based on the earliest (or latest) a task can *start*, and the earliest (or latest) it can *finish*, you will be able to manipulate the schedule to optimize your project. For example, you might see that the walk is better in phase I, or you might catch the movie by moving that task to phase II, and save money on the early show.

The best way to do this is to draw arrows between the tasks, and give it a test drive. For example, drawing an arrow from the gym to the movie, then to the grocery store will give you a more visual look, which is also another merit of the Critical Path Method.

Ensure that you put down the Critical Path Method visually on paper. And as mentioned above, give it clarity. You will see this as a prerequisite to being a Life Wizard, and practice Perfect Life Management. You must give things clarity on paper. And then you feel like a true Life Wizard, because as if by magic, *vague things become clear objectives.*

Breaking it Down

When you awoke from slumber this morning, you brushed your teeth, had breakfast, took a shower, and conducted many other tasks, with the ultimate objective of getting dressed in the morning. The quintessence spirit of these tasks was the Work Breakdown Structure (WBS). You took one big objective, and broke down all the tasks necessary to meet that objective in small manageable tasks.

Of course, this is the epitome of simplicity in presenting WBS. But it clearly demonstrates that by using WBS, whatever the daunting object that may be haunting you can be exorcised. WBS is also used in breaking down tasks into many manageable mini tasks.

Not all your projects will require you to have WBS, but I strongly suggest that you use WBS in important projects, such as applying for a home loan. As is the case with many projects, many different people or even groups, may come together to form the complete objective. The Life Wizard must give the WBS a sturdy structure. WBS is broken down in two arrangements, Functional and Chronological.

Although we can use both the structures in any given WBS, only one is chosen as the main structure, and the other is selected as its subset. For example, if we select the Functional WBS Structure as our main structure to work with in the WBS, then we will choose the Chronological WBS Structure as the subset, and vice versa.

The reason we use the term subset is because logically, both the elements, function and time, will be present in any given WBS structure that you follow. It is a matter of giving the one more weight, over the other.

FUNCTIONAL WBS STRUCTURE

In the Functional WBS Structure, the WBS is broken down first by function, then by timeline. Timeline is the view of the project, or your objective, which accentuates the interval of times with respect to the tasks, or the sub-tasks. In this case, we are giving more importance to the function, then the timeline, as far as the layouts of the tasks are concerned.

The fist step in the Functional WBS Structure is to break down the tasks by the different categories, then arrange the functions in a vertical order. The Functional Structure looks like a tree trunk, with the functions to be performed in the tasks are lined up from the top to the bottom. Can you picture it? Each function can be further broken down to detail of your comfort. We will take a look at an example in a moment.

But first, let us define Chronological WBS Structure:

CHRONOLOGICAL WBS STRUCTURE

The basic concept for the Chronological WBS Structure is the same as the Functional WBS Structure. However, if you feel that time is of the matter in a particular project, consider the Chronological WBS Structure. Chronological WBS Structure, as you might imagine, is more sensitive to time. Hence, it stands to reason that this structure will be laid out according to the timeline.

Just like the Functional WBS Structure, the tasks are lined up, and visually at first it starts to look like a trunk. But as the tasks are edged in, according to the order of their execution, as more then one task may start at any one given time, they start to overlap, and eventually the Chronological WBS structure looks more like a timetable, then just a structure.

It will benefit us now to take a look at an example:

HOME LOAN WBS

Lets assume that you are preparing to buy a house. The disquiet objective of successfully applying for a loan looms over you. In fact, let me take you through the process of a typical example.

You start out by having the thought of a new house initiate somewhere in your mind. Maybe it was a suggestion planted by your life partner, or perhaps you decided that it was time to move up. At first you are amused with the idea, then even a bit entertained, as you and start looking at the possibilities in newspapers, and even doing a drive-by of some new neighborhoods.

In your excitement you make a few phone calls to some agents. Quickly, it dawns on you that you need a systematic approach, as phone calls from agents, possible sellers, and other mediators and representatives, who would like to get in the action, inundate you.

This is the case, where you would experiment with both, Functional and Chronological Structures.

You start organizing it in your mind. The object gives way to a loosely based process, which gives way to more confusion, if not a light panic, as the vastness of the project creeps on you with an overwhelming sensation. In a fervent attempt, by a call of fanatical reasoning, if not by an involuntary mechanical process, you start scribbling on a piece of paper.

You have now in your hands, a loose version of WBS.

You recall the Functional Structure of WBS, and you start scribbling even more. But this time it is taking shape of a logical process, based on the categories that must be satisfied, in order for you to secure the loan.

You make the following structure:

HOME LOAN FUNCTIONAL STRUCTURE OF WBS

Category One—Reconnaissance and Exploration

Study the general neighborhood

Survey the price range

Research and analyze financial feasibility

Browse individual houses

Category Two—Contacts

Real Estate Agent

Financial Agent

Real Estate Lawyer

Inspector

Appraiser

Movers

Category Three—Real Estate Agent Functions

Acquire listings

See properties

Synchronize with Real Estate Lawyer and Financial Agent

Assist in closing

Category Four—Finance Functions

Acquire credit report

Correct credit aberrations

Negotiate loan points

Deliver financing

Category Five—Real Estate Lawyer Functions

Check property documentation

Communicate with Real Estate Lawyer of the selling party

Assist in closing

Category Six—Inspector and Appraiser Functions

Inspect property

Appraise property

Category Seven—Logistics

Select house

Coordinate with the appropriate parties for closing

Coordinate with the movers for move date

Conduct moving activities

Coordinate with utilities

Secure city permits and formalities

HOME LOAN CHRONOLOGICAL STRUCTURE OF WBS

Jan 1–Jan 15

Study the general neighborhood

Real Estate Agent contact

Acquire listings

See properties

Jan 16–Jan 31

Survey the price range

Research and analyze financial feasibility

Browse individual houses

Select house

Feb 1–Feb 15

Financial Agent contact

Real Estate Lawyer contact

Synchronize Real Estate Agent with Real Estate Lawyer and Financial Agent

Feb 16–Feb 28

Select house

Acquire credit report

Correct credit aberrations

Negotiate loan points

Communicate with Real Estate Lawyer of the selling party

Check property documentation

Contact inspector, appraiser, and movers

Mar 1–Mar 15

Inspect property

Appraise property

Deliver financing

Close on property

Coordinate with utilities

Secure city permits and formalities

Coordinate with the movers for move date

Conduct moving activities

As you practice WBS with different events in your life, you will notice that some will repeat itself; especially, if they are not the major life changing events, as moving to a new house. You may find it useful to use it for less influencing events, such as many activities that you do occasionally. For example, a while ago, I mentioned my trips to the library. Considering that I spend a massive portion of my free time in the libraries, having a WBS helps me.

Remember that the main purpose of WBS is to break down the major objective into easily digestible pieces. And if it helps you to do that with undemanding things like going to the grocery store, then I would encourage you to use it.

In my case, for many years now, I have made lists for many activities. A good example is the grocery store. Many of us have grocery lists, but mine has categories, and sometimes…sub-categories. Does that remind you of Functional WBS Structure? This is not overkill, and it has a great positive impact in the efficient way I can execute daily activities.

For example, instead of just having a grocery list, have a Functional WBS Structure. Base the functions on the way your local grocery store is divided. Have the sections that you encounter as you walk in as the first category, and the rest of them, according to their appearance, as you walk along with your shopping cart. I have used this system for many years, and I can safely say that I never forget anything, and I never have to back track anywhere.

DYNAMIC WBS VS. STATIC WBS

When you use WBS for minor events, such as library visits and grocery stores, you will notice a certain repetition of tasks. If you see that your

WBS is identical every week, or every time that particular activity is executed, then perhaps it will be a good idea to use the same WBS every time. Hence, you will convert a Dynamic WBS to a Static WBS.

I suppose the above is an argument for using WBS for minor events, although it stands to good ground that WBS for major events is indispensable.

The Buying Game

B udgets are helpful for the smallest things. You must realize that as you put into practice Life Wizard's Perfect Life Management, you will find it exceedingly useful for implementing the techniques and methodology presented in this book. As the days go by, you will come to a realization that even though you knew the fundamental essence of it, having a methodology to give it structure increases the realistic chance that you will put the technique to a good use.

Budgets are a good example of this. Every time we plan to part with our money, we have a budget. But do we really use the budget? And if so, to what extent do we even think about it?

When you have a need to buy a microwave, do you go to the store, with a rough estimate of how much you will be spending, and just buy it? We know that many of us do. As a matter of fact, how many of us have done this with even bigger purchases? Here is the danger; even if you are sophisticated enough in the art of budgeting, you have to be continuously be aware of the actual budget making process, or it will slip by you.

In fact, I did it just a few years ago. I used to drive a sports car, which like many sports car, was a rear wheel drive. This was a constant threat for me during the winters in the Midwest. Many times I had the excitement of experiencing my car do a complete 180-degree turn on the freeway, without any input from me!

One evening, after one of those hair-raising experiences, I was so fed up that I decided to buy a car from the first dealer I saw on the Internet, which, thankfully, in this case was a Saturn dealer. I called up the dealer with the intention of buying the car the same night. I was somewhat confident that in the back of my mind I had the exact figure of my potential expenditure.

My goal was to walk in the dealership and announce, "I have $3000 for down payment, and I will not pay a penny over $200 a month". As I walked in the salesperson's office, and announced my requirements, to my great surprise, he said, "okay". I walked out of there with a 1999 Saturn.

In the frame of four hours, I had made a decision to buy a car, walked in the dealership, and walked out with a car.

You might look upon quick decisions as an admirable quality. And yes, even I thought I had done great. But when we look at the budget process, you will see how much more advantages it is to go through the actual exercise.

Many of us fail to see the most important fact that purchasing something is not just the act of giving some body else our money, and getting something in return, in other words it is not just a simple case of *quid pro quo* (something for something).

There is really nothing too much wrong with that, except that there is absolutely no planning to back your decision. And you are loosing out on a rich experience of budget planning, which could save you thousands of dollars on big decisions, as well as make your preference win over everybody else's.

With that in mind, we can elaborate a bit on the objectives of the budget. The most obvious objective is so that we remain within our financial resources. But there are two other major advantages to doing budgets like a pro, which are:

1. Making better decisions

2. Justifying your purchase to others

We can satisfy both of these advantages by following the Life Wizard methodology for making every purchase. The idea hire is to make a logical decision, just as a professional manager would in making any purchase. We will use the simple case of purchasing a new big screen TV (my favorite) as an example:

BUDGET ANALYSIS PROCESS

The following is the outline of a budget:

1) Cost & Benefit Analysis

    a) Benefit

        i) Intangible Benefits

        ii) Tangible Benefits

    b) Costs

        i) Initial Costs

        ii) Ongoing Costs

    c) Projected Payback

2) Budget Assessment

We will take a look at the different components of the Budget, and make an actual budget of the big screen TV.

The Cost & Benefit Analysis has been broken down in two sections, Costs and Benefits. The Benefits, in turn, are also divided into two sections, Intangible Benefits and Tangible Benefits.

Intangible Benefits are those benefits, which cannot be explained, in concrete physical terms, such as "acquiring greater satisfaction of sound experience form the system." Tangible Benefits, conversely, can be explained in actual terms, such as "two 50 inch Speakers".

The Costs are also divided into two parts, Initial Costs and Ongoing Costs. The Initial Costs will be the actual cost of the TV and its components, as well as delivery, and anything else that is associated with actually acquiring the TV, bringing it home, and start using it. The

Ongoing Costs are those costs, which are required for the continuous operation of the TV, such as the electric bill.

Projected Payback is the amount of time it takes for the new system to payback the costs of the project. This part is hard to express in Life Management, as the budgets are not designed to make money. But with a little imagination, something could be written for this category. For example, you can display that the household saved $800 in movie tickets, due to the movie-like experience of the big screen TV. Hence, in combination with other items in this category, and given enough years, the payback can be justified.

Budget Assessment is a careful review of your personal finances. This is separate from the Cost & Benefit Analysis, because the former only takes into account, as the name suggests, the costs and benefits of the project (purchase). But there comes a point in the decision process, where you have to officially bring out the check book, and realistically define the condition and the affordably of the purchase.

Based on the above considerations of the analysis, let's take a look at the actual budget:

BUDGET FOR THE SONY 65" WIDESCREEN HDTV/PROJECTION TV
MODEL: SON KDP-65XBR2

COST & BENEFIT ANALYSIS

Intangible Benefits:

- Relaxed disposition every evening after enjoying the product

- Increased popularity in the neighborhood

- Escalation in social status amongst friends and family

- Reduction in travel time in going back and forth to movie theaters

- Enhanced audio visual experience

- Additional motivation for a family gathering

  Tangible Benefits:

- Annual savings in movie tickets: $800

- Annual savings in other entertainment, by staying home, as a direct result of having this product at home: $1,400

- Annual savings in fuel and other transport costs: $200

- Annual savings in other expenses, as a direct result of having this product at home, such as reduction of computer games, novels, and other distractedly entertainment: $900

- Total Tangible Benefit: $3,300

  Initial Costs:

- TV, warranty, and taxes: $5,600

- Delivery: $200

- Total Initial Costs: $5,800

  Ongoing Costs:

- Annual utility charges: $200

- Total Ongoing Costs: $200

  Total Costs: $6,000

  Projected Payback:

- Total project costs over two years: $6,200 ($200 in utility charges is an annual expense, hence $200 x 2= $400 then, $5,800 + $400 = $6,200)

- Total benefits over two years: $6,600.

Hence, the payback period is approximately two years

Budget Assessment is a personal activity. Use the meeting skills, if you think that the Budget Assessment is at borderline, and there may be some members, who are not enthusiastic about acquiring the big screen TV. Once all the family members approve the budget, then use the other Perfect Life Management skills outlined in this book, such as the Work Breakdown Structure and the Critical Path Method.

Stencils of Life

You can save many hours of labor trying to reinvent information-gathering documents by using templates. Templates are kind of stencils, which have certain placeholders of information that you collect on a regular basis. For example, a common template we saw earlier was for Status Report. There are many other templates that you can use, depending on your current objectives. For this reason, I have included some common templates used in the corporate world, and the explanations of the fields that are filled out.

There is another rather important reason that the templates should be used. Templates, when filled with words, create a record for your protection. Besides creating a stencil for articulating your objectives, it documents people, actions, responsibilities, and accountabilities.

During the times in our lives, when we undertake major projects, sometimes we loose perceptive of things. We become complacent. Even if you are one of those vigilant souls, there is still a risk of being overwhelmed. We saw in the case of purchasing the house, even at an outline level, there are numerous tasks that have to be performed, just to get the basics prepared for execution.

And the biggest danger is when you put all of this together. When you take a bit of complacency, a dash of being overwhelmed, and a tad of overlooking of some significant facts. During these times of exact laws, and frequent lawsuits, you have to protect yourself. This is not to sound paranoid and mistrustful of others, but many times I have caught myself in the self-delusion that there is nobody lurking out there in the realm of possibilities to harm me, or my family.

Unfortunately, this self-delusion can be self-destructive. Especially when we hold ourselves in the highest order of honor and honesty. We feel that we are loving, caring, honest, and reciprocally attract similar attributes from the ones we love and trust, and that all is well. Except that there is a small amount of people out there, who do not share this goodness reciprocation theory with you. Let me illustrate this very important point by sharing with you what Leo Nikolayevich Tolstoy wrote in Book One of "War and Peace".

The character, Count Rostov, was fighting the French in a battle. During a break in action, when all seemed quite, Rostov lost a bit of his composure, and began to feel complacent, or perhaps he was overwhelmed by the whole engagement. He saw people, who were obviously not his men, running toward him with bayonets drawn. Here are his thoughts that Tolstoy wrote, "Who are they? Are they coming at me? Can they be running at me? And why? To kill me? *Me* whom everyone is so fond of? He thought of his mother's love for him, of his family's and his friends', and the enemy's intention of killing him seemed impossible."

It is all too common to be in an environment of comfort and loose track of just a few things, which may cause much trouble in the future. By design of others, by not able to follow through on certain tasks, or just by wasting precious time, when attempting the same projects in the future. Templates are there to give you structure and information. It is there to protect you, so you can follow through from the beginning of a project, to the very end, even years from now. You can do things with the best of intentions, but you never know, what others have in store for you.

A list and brief description is presented, followed by a more detailed look at each template:

1. Gap analysis

   1.1. Identifies the "gap" between your current status and your final objective

2. Resource Analysis

2.1. An inventory of the resources that you have access to for the journey toward your objective

3. Issue log

3.1. Documents the issues you have had in your activities

3.1.1. Issue escalation

3.1.1.1. Provides an avenue of escalating the issue

4. Change Request

4.1. Documents major changes to avoid unnecessary extra work and to hold others accountable for their promises

5. Communications Plan

6. Post Project Checklist

6.1. After a project is done, a check is filled out to ensure that all the angles have been covered

GAP ANALYSIS

Gap Analysis is essentially a tool to examine where you are, where you want to go, and what is the disparity between the two points. The following are the fields common to the Gap Analysis.

Current Situation: This could be a thing, a process, or any other objective already achieved. Your purpose is to list it, and examine these items. Your current situation may not be just one thing, but a collection of items. For example, your current situation may contain people, equipment, and material. It is important to remember that the current situation be broken down to the appropriate granularity. For example, don't just consider people, but also organizations.

Final Situation: This is easier to document then the current situation, as this is your final destination. Once again, it is important to consider the granularity and the combination of things.

Gap: Arriving to the gap can be a lot of fun, or very disheartening, depending on how you did in your goal manifesting process. If you did it with faith and conviction, then you cannot wait till you document this gap, so you can see exactly what needs to be done. On the other hand, if you perceive your objective as an unrealistic goal, then you are doomed.

RESOURCE ANALYSIS

A Resource Analysis is important to conduct, as it shows you a bird's eye view of all your resources, as well as illustrates somewhat of a timeline of the their utilization.

Resource List: A simple list of your resources. List people, equipment, and facilities. For example, you can list your Real Estate Agent here, as well as the fax machine, and your home office.

Involvement Phase: This is the phase where you will identify when the resources will become active in the project.

Resource Contribution: List of contribution that the resource will be making. Keep at a high level, and list only the major contribution, such as Legal Advice. Do not list inanimate objects here, such as fax machines.

Involvement Level: Take an educated guess on the level of involvement of a resource. You can be specific and list the actual high-level task of the resource.

Resource Cost: This is one of the important fields in this template. Besides the obvious benefit of using this information for budget purposes, you can document any estimates that may be given to you by the resource. For example, fee estimates by Home Inspectors.

Resource cost Analysis Comment: Once you have a clear documentation of the resource, you may do a Cost & Benefit Analysis, like we did on the budget section, on this particular resource, to determine the value of retaining this individual resource.

ISSUE LOG

During an activity, which is complex enough to go several days, such as major, there will certainly be instances, where the immediate resolution is not known. Mark these items as "issues" and document them. An instance is an Issue, if it meets one of the following conditions:

- There is no resource to resolve a condition. For example, The finance person requires a certain credit rating, and you do not think that your credit report will meet those terms. This, of course, would be a major issue, if you were buying a car or a home.

- There is a discrepancy about the person responsible to solve an issue. For example, you think that your son has been designated as a resource to take the trash out this week, and he has different ideas.

- An issue arises, but the solution may not be in effect for several weeks, or months (in this case, the Issue Log is used as a "place holder" for issues so they do not get "lost").

The fields that make up an Issue log consist of the following:

Issue Name: Give the Issue a name for better tracking. For example, "Credit Deficiency".

Issue Description: Short description of the Issue.

Issue Date: Date the issue was *discovered*.

Issue Resolution: What would be the ideal resolution of this Issue?

Issue Responsibility: In your opinion, who is responsible for this Issue's resolution?

Issue Escalation: Issue Escalation provides you with an avenue of taking your issue the next level up. For example, if you have an issue with a certain action of the seller of the house, your first obvious action would be to go and address the seller. However, just in case, the issue does not get resolved, then the Issue Escalation will spell out for you the next level. For instance, in this case, the escalation of issue might be to the lawyer.

Issue Priority: Use standard priority codes, such as C = Critical, H = High, M = Medium, or L = Low

Issue Status: Use standard status codes, such as O = Open, H = Hold, and C = Closed

CHANGE CONTROL

Change Control is another way you can keep some control on the events, and to some extent, the actions of other participants in any project. Change Control essentially cruises the established project baseline, which you can use as a guide to ensure that there are no major changes in the project.

If there are a lot of people and resources involved in the undertaking, expectations and requirements get *added* to the project. Soon, if you do not take care of it, things seem to creep out of your control, and overwhelm you; thus, affecting you and the end objectives in an adverse manner. This phenomenon is called Scope Creep.

Change Control battles Scope Creep by tracking fields that alerts the Life Manager, when Scope Creep is eminent. The fields are designed to look at anything, which raises the workload of any resource.

It is important to remember that Change Control is not traditionally used to *stop* the Scope Creep, but to document it, so there is clarity on the scope of the project, and the possible reassignment of the tasks.

Some of the common fields are described below:

Change Control Name: Assign a name to the Change, so you can track it later.

Change Description: Short description of the Change.

Change Date: Date the Change was documented.

Effect on Project: This is the most important part of Change Control. The rest of the fields are used only to document the Changes, but this field will document the exact consequence on the project, due to *a* particular Change. For example, if you get an indication from the selling party that they might be inclined to move the closing date, then that is an entry for Change Control.

Or, any change in a previously agreed upon accord.

A good example is when we purchased our house; the house inspector indicated that there was a slight gas leak in the laundry room. I immediately made a note of it in the Issue Log. It was agreed upon that the sellers would call the gas company, and have it fixed by an approved source. Well, it turned out that the seller did not go to the approved source to repair the gas leak. We saw the evidence of which in the laundry room. Hence, the entry in the Change Control was the fact that an approved professional did not remedy the problem.

It so happened that in a few weeks henceforth, the gas started to leak again, and we had to spend some money having it fixed by an approved professional. I retrieved the Change Control documentation, and the lawyer was able to acquire us the remedy by billing the final fix to the sellers.

COMMUNICATIONS PLAN

Communications Plan helps you document the intricacies of the way the communications will flow. When things are in full swing in your life, and there are multiple people involved, you must have a written record of who will talk to whom, and the frequency of those events.

This will help you find out, if there is a lapse of responsibility, or a delay in something, and you can then determine, if you need to step in and take charge of the situation.

Communications Plan for Life Management will have the following fields:

Sender: The person who will initiate the communication. For example, once your credit is approved, the finance company will initiate a document, such as the "Pre-Approval" papers, to the Real Estate Agent.

Receiver: The person who will receive the communiqué from the Sender, in this case the Real Estate Agent.

Intent: The intent of the communication. This is important to document, because sometimes we get wind of the many different promises, made in a flurry by many different people, at the beginning of a venture. Sometimes the intent of the communication is indigenous to the particular professional domain, and this field will keep you enlightened at all times. For example, do you know the difference between a Pre-Approval document and a Pre-Qualification document?

Frequency: There may be communications that may be performed more then once. For example, if you have arranged a particular project, which requires Status Reports, then you may denote the frequency of such a report, such as "weekly update", or "every other Thursday".

Method: Most of the time, you do not have any control on the method of communication, but it will be good to have a documentation of the method. For example, the method of communicating the Pre-Approval document may be by fax.

POST PROJECT CHECKLIST

The Post Project Checklist is designed to ensure that you met with all your objectives that you set out with, in a particular project. The following are some of the fields to consider:

- Summary of Objectives: It helps to rewrite your main objectives in a project, to make sure that you achieved all of them successfully.

- Leftover Tasks: As with any major project, you will always have some loose ends. It is important to document these so you do not loose track of them.

- People Involved: From the person that came to check the foundation, to the Real Estate Agent, keep a list of each person's tasks, and their contact number, for future references.

- Document Control: Ensure that all the documents have been accounted for and properly filled. These include even minor things, such as the warranty for the garage door opener.

- Lessons Learned: I can almost guarantee that no matter how many times you take up a particular project; there will always be some contingencies that you can learn from. Document these and learn from them.

Organization

The process of organizations has been the basis of thought. Aristotle used it to define the basic structure of his philosophy. His method contained some basic elements for the organization, which is intriguing because he focused on the *structure* of organization, and not the actual process.

To further elucidate, we are interested in the final structure and the *function* the organization will perform for us, mundane organizational structures, providing striking results, such as a filing system.

I am concentrating on organization because it is so basic, and yet we are not so compelled to embrace it, or to at least give it enough weight in our everyday activities. It is not my intention to allude to such organizations as an administrative structure, or a managerial structure. But the structure of *thought* before any other thought, as in the case of methodological thinking.

As soon as a thought enters your mind, do you *think* about it? Do you ponder where it came from? Do you attempt to backtrack your thoughts to trace it? Do you see where it is going? Do you let it flee, or try and stop it?

The organization of thought can be quite different in each of our minds, depending on how much effort we put in to organize it. And it *is* an effort, but with practice you can have a sort of a hierarchy in the way your thoughts flow.

This is really the beginning of being a Life Wizard, of practicing Life Management, as how you organize your thoughts is how you will organize the activities. Without proper organizing, all you have is pandemonium, and what begins with disarray and turmoil has little hope to be efficient.

Unfortunately there is a widespread misleading conception that we can thrive in chaos. An unorganized mind can get things done. But this is a fallacy. Once you have tackled this section, you may draw your own conclusions.

Recently, while talking to a friend, I was argued upon that order or chaos, the results come out the same. Somehow things are shaken up, like popcorn in a bag, to even out the outcome. That is the first lesson in the Organization theory, things are not that simple, as humble inanimate objects coming together with the mere perfunctory act of shaking something.

It is a deliberate and premeditated effort of the mind. And that is not entirely easy, as premeditation is required, which means that the mind has to be alert of receiving thoughts, not just merely reacting to them.

Back to the argumentative friend now. Some traffic lights in her neighborhood were the incongruent nature of our thoughts. She contended that given enough tries, regardless of the traffic signals presence, or not, the average time of her commute to work would be the same, or almost the same. Her main assertion was that organization does not create a structure it is credited with.

I am not presenting this case because it has a significance of great implications, but how people in their everyday activities so casually ignore the influence of organization. Not in just a few things, but almost everything.

Nevertheless, once the traffic signals were out of order, or perhaps not functioning for one reason or the other. The end result was that it took her twice the time to get to work.

Now, one can make the argument here that perhaps the longer time of commute was attributed to the fact that the commuters were used to the traffic signs. And they simply reacted to the situation of not having their familiar traffic signals and possibly took some irrational action; thereby causing the delays.

And that is exactly my point. We are intrinsically depended on organizational thoughts and pattern that it projects outside our bodies. The mere expression of disorder in just one instance has a ripple effect on many entities. In this case the expression of the traffic signal of being "out of order" caused the many motorists to be sequentially disorderly. Once again, it is not the occurrence that is in question, but the aggregate view of organization. It is not the individual conduct of the motorists that we are questioning, but the fact that the disorganization of something caused an unwanted reaction.

THOUGHT TRACE-BACK

Once we loop back to the fact that the one occasion of an event sends an essence of instability to the whole structure, whatever that might be an activity you are looking at as a project, or a one-time happening. Hence, we have to take acute measures, when we experience these events.

It must be pointed out that the one time event may be a repetition of a series of events, in some variance. This may give it an appearance of the event as a one-time event, which is even a greater reason for us to be intensely alert of such measures.

Take for example, the mundane event of filing away documents. The one instance, of receiving a correspondence in the mail, and subsequently the act of filing of that mail in a predetermined location is an event in organization. If it is not filed properly, then the consequences can be trifling annoyance, if it is a minor invoice for a trivial purchase, to major tribulations, if it is an important time sensitive official document.

At this point in our discussion, allow me now take you back one step. Before you get the opportunity to do the filing. If fact, we have to be a bit more generic, when we rationalize the process of Thought Trace-Back.

In order to think, you have to process a thought. In order to process that thought it must be in existence in your mind; and in order to be in existence in your mind, the thought has to enter it. The point at which the thought enters your mind, the thought must be organized. If it is not, it will take a life of its own, and create chaos in your mind.

The daunting task, which I just described to you, is not as intimidating. It will take a bit of practice, in the topic of our section, of tracing back the thought. The phrase Trace-Back is used, because it is presumed that in the beginning stages of mind organization, the thought may escape your guards, and slip in to its own agenda. Actually, even after years of practice, depending on what your preoccupation is at the time of thought-entry, it may still escape you. Hence, we have to do our best to contain and trace-back the thought.

The Thought Trace-Back process is quite precise in its description. The process involves you to acknowledge a thought, and trace it back to its origin. For example, during a recent drive to Palatine, Illinois, I had a sudden urge to eat sushi. I immediately put the *brakes* on the flow of thoughts. That is the first step. I then began to carefully think to what I was thinking, or watching, or listening to, as I drove. That is the second step.

I quickly realized that I was just listening to the some Japanese music on the radio, and that reminded me that my cousin was in Tokyo that week. Which in turn reminded me of Japanese food, and consequently I inadvertently started thinking of my favorite food, which happens to be sushi. And given that my favorite sushi bar is in Palatine, Illinois, my *yen* for sushi was manifested as the final thought.

But here is a delicate detour to the straight path of Thought Trace-Back. There may be other stimulus that may be instinctively nudging you toward the final thought. This supplementary thought, which originates as a result of the possible bonus stimulus, may be in amalgamation of some other thought, or may act autonomously. Whichever the case, it will be wise to search for other thoughts, caused by other stimuli, which may be present. In this case, the bonus stimulus was the location, which was the Village of Palatine, which also happens to host my favorite restaurant, The Pacific Buffet.

On the face of it, the above example may not hold too much weight in the broader Life Management structure. But I value it, as it illustrates the Thought Trace-Back well. As I hold the act of such humdrum activities as eating, sleeping, and relaxing a major part of life, and thus a major part of being a true Life Wizard, and a major part of Life Management.

We can now move to a bit more apt example of Thought Trace-Back. Recently, when I was shopping for cars, I found myself attracted to an overpriced sedan, which I would have never thought of purchasing, previous to my physically approaching the car. "What is attracting me to this car?" my mind whirled. I immediately deployed step one, and hushed my mind, so I can reflect on the dominant thought. I then carefully evaluated my surrounding to search for the prevailing stimulus.

I noticed that my eyes were quite forcefully focused on the wide luxurious tan leather seats of the sedan. I then traced back my thoughts to just a few seconds ago, thinking of the lavish first class seat of an airliner that I had recently been fortunate enough to experience. Outside stimulus, in combination with your present thoughts, can be a powerful and extreme blend.

So how does this influence the organization? Well, to start with what you did above was a practice of organizing your thoughts in the proper sequence.

By carefully analyzing your thought pattern flow, both forward and backward, you are able to control what your next thought is going to be. In essence, you are creating your own filing cabinet in your mind, as you determine *what* thoughts get arranged *where*.

Hence, the three steps of the Thought Trace-Back can be defined as follows:

1. Quite your mind, and focus on the prevailing thought

2.   Search for the dominant stimulus/stimuli

3.   Organize your thoughts in the direction you want

If we were the only ones involved in all our activities in our lives, we could stop here. But we all know that we continually dodge ideas, suggestions, orders, commands, instructions, and manipulations from others. Therefore, it would stand to reason to have a section of this methodology to stretch in to the domain of others.

We will now examine the possibilities of mind control, or to be a bit less diabolic, thought organizations in other people's minds.

MIND CONTROL

Once again I venture in the realm of such unhallowed flavors, which may conjure up images of a sinister magician brainwashing its subjects to his indulgences. In its most pure form, of course, not mind control, but a certain ability to *control* the organization of someone's thoughts. I suppose one could have a thought regarding this or that, and have someone else slightly alter the course of those thoughts by mentioning something. Or to go even a step further and suggest that suppose one could have a thought, and it can be altered by mere introduction to an external stimuli.

In a concentrated form, it is quite the same as the Thought Trace-Back Method, but the external stimulus, which alters the dominant thought, could be you. Hence, perhaps creating a new path for that new, or altered, thought. Would that be then mind control? We are not, of course, interested in mind control, but purely in organizing of those thoughts to *control* the instance of a moment, or an event, as it relates and ultimately affects your project, or activity.

The question then arises, "*How* does one interject an external stimulus that would get the result of Thought Trace-Back in somebody else's mind?" One could simply *tell* the other person. But that is not too effective as now the other person knows clearly that you are *telling* him/

her. You are not there to teach, as your purpose is not to *teach* organization to this person. But rather to have the person organize certain information, which will give a desired result.

Keeping this end result in mind, we call upon one of our past Philosophers; perhaps one of the earliest examples of Western Philosophy. We call upon the teacher of Plato, and indirectly the teacher of Aristotle. We call upon Socrates. But the paradoxical phenomenon here is that Socrates did not teach Plato and Aristotle. In fact, he did not teach anybody. Or for that matter, wrote anything. *He asked questions.*

So in essence, Socrates taught by asking, instead of telling. He professed ignorance of the truth of the matter under discussions. As the conversation continued, he asked more and more questions to unfold the truth, and thus taught the *student* the lesson. His goal was to teach what he assumed was goodness and virtue. We, on the other hand, do not have such high soaring goals. Our aim is to just organize the thoughts of the person, whom we are engaged with in conversation.

But it is important to ponder the preceding Socratic Method, as we will use part of it in what I call the Ajacratic Method. It may seem pretentious, as I so obviously used my own name to define it, but I had to give it *some* name. I find it useful to give things names. We will, to a certain extent, use the slightly sneaky, but subtle and very powerful way of Socrates. We will use the questions, to organize thoughts.

It will be up to you to introduce a stimulus to the other party. By reading the section about the Thought Trace-Back, you know how the outside stimulus works. But this will work only if you are not trying to manipulate the other person in any major way, but are instead trying to enlighten him/her to your way of thinking.

But above all remember the dual propose of Thought Trace-Back. It is to organize the thoughts to achieve certain point, at the same time, *due to the organization*, achieve the goal in the most efficient manner.

Consider the following conversation between a car dealer and me. Here is the setting:

The car dealer, we will call him Honest Ed, has the car on his lot. He is willing and quite persuasive in having me take the car home, and try it out for a few days, as I am not quite sure about the purchase. I, on the other hand, know that once I drive the car off the lot, there are a number of variables that can make the decision to take the car home a very bad one indeed.

If I tell him my reasons, I will have to categorize it for him to convince him of the reasons, and as he is a professional salesperson, I doubt that I can win a shootout with him. Hence, I decided to ask him key questions, so he can organize thoughts in his mind, as I have it organized in mine. Keeping in mind that I have a dual purpose here:

1. To have the thoughts organize in Honest Ed's mind to suit my objectives

2. To also ensure that there is some organization taking place Honest Ed's mind, so when I decide to purchase the car, I am offered the most efficient process and service

Honest Ed: Shaun, take the car home.

Shaun: But I have not paid for it yet.

Honest Ed: Not a problem Shaun. Your credit is good with us. When you decide **(Shaun's comment: Notice he said *when* and not *if*. As you use your methods, you have to be aware of your opponent's methods, as well)** to buy the car, just bring it back, and we will do the paperwork. You can keep the car for three days.

Shaun: So I can just drive the car out of here?

Honest Ed: Yep.

Shaun: Is the car insured?

Honest Ed: Well…The car is insured, but your insurance will have to cover it.

Shaun: Why?

Honest Ed: Well…Just in case…Something happens to the car.

Shaun: Like what?

Honest Ed: Well…I don't want to be pessimistic, so I really don't want to say stuff.

Shaun: Well, I am not in this business, and as you probably have other potential buyers drive the car home before purchase. So I figured that you might have some knowledge, based on prior occurrences **(Shaun's comment: Notice that I am trying to use the Socratic Method to *unfold* the truth)**, about what could go wrong. For example, maybe you can tell me what has happened to the cars in the past, even if the chances of those happenings are rare.

Honest Ed: Well, in the past, we have had a person have an accident…A minor one.

Shaun: He had to pay?

Honest ED: Yes…Well, his insurance did.

Shaun: Car ever been stolen?

Honest Ed: Yes…Once…Twice, I think.

Shaun: Stolen? Really? My Goodness! And the guy had to pay.

Honest Ed: Like I said, the insurance does.

Shaun: Hmmmmm. Okay, what if I do not like the car? I can just drive it back and walk away?

Honest Ed: Absolutely. We return the deposit back.

Shaun: Deposit?

Honest Ed: Yes, a goodwill deposit.

Shaun: And I get that back, as soon as I drop off the car?

Honest Ed: No, we mail you the check.

Shaun: Hmmmm…Anybody report any family problems?

Honest Ed: Family problems?

Shaun: Yes. You know, the guy drives the car home, the wife does not like it, one kid likes it, the other does not, some want to keep it, the others do not, wife complains about the deposit not being returned, stuff like that. Any family problems reported?

Honest Ed: Oh yeah, all the time hahahaha. But…eh…It is usually resolved…Quickly

Shaun: Wow, you know, I never knew that I could have so many hassles. I think that if I take the car home, and I get any negative feedback, or have any hassle, I really don't think that I would want to buy this car; even though I quite like it. I think that I will pass on taking it home, but I will take the test drive.

Based on the above conversation, we used the Ajacratic Method not to educate or expose a revelation to Honest Ed, but to *drive a point across*. Now when I suggested that I would just settle for a test drive, his opposition to the idea is benign, as we helped him organize his thoughts. Also, going back to the Socratic Method, notice that we professed a certain amount of ignorance, to facilitate the illusion that this was not all a huge facade on my part.

We also spoke of organizing Honest Ed's mind for him. What did we exactly do to him? The following are the thought organizational hierarchy for Honest Ed's mind, preceding the Ajacratic Method line of questioning:

Show Car—Test Drive Car—Take Car Home—Buy Car

And my thought organizational hierarchy was:

See Car—Test Drive Car

We poked some holes in Honest Ed's thought organizational hierarchy, and thus first created some doubts, and conclusively organized it to our liking:

Show Car—Test Drive Car—Take Car Home???—Buy Car???

To finally:

Show Car—Test Drive Car

While rearranging of the thought organizational hierarchy can be used effectively, there remains a section to discuss the byproduct of the reorganized thoughts, which gives way to a more organized way of living.

THE SYSTEM

As we talked about organizing the thoughts in some form in our minds, at some point it flows out of it. When the organization of the information in our mind *itself* is not our final objective, then some other functions must be performed. In this premise, a good example would be a typical filing system that you may come across in any business.

You cannot walk in any successful business and not see a filing system. You may see an absence of it in just an arbitrarily chosen workstation, but those who are responsible in keeping track of records and other accounts, will never be caught without it. Well, when we put this conception adjacent to your personal life, you will clearly see that you are that person now, who is completely responsible in keeping track of all your personal accounts.

Even if you only get one piece of document in a week, you must organize and discipline your mind enough to accomplish a good filing system. If you have never employed a good filing system before, it will be a bit difficult for you to set up one right away. But you must start on this track.

In some ways the whole organizational ecosystem is a loop. If you do not follow with the fundamentals, such as the Thought Trace-Back, you cannot have enough discipline and order to be organized. But on the other hand, if you do not immediately make a decision to be *physically* organized, you will never have enough calm and control of your mind to be *mentally* organized.

Hence, to put this all in some kind of a package, I would like to ask you to do a very simple thing to accommodate the Perfect Life Management in your life. I would like to ask you to establish a very simple filing system in your personal life.

Here is the structure that you will follow:

First, determine the number of people in your family, who may be inclined to use the system. For example, if you have a wife, and two kids above ten years of age, then your number is four.

Second, add two to that number, hence your number now is six.

Third, designate at least six drawers in a room, which is NOT your bedroom, for your filing system.

Fourth, allocate the drawers, also will be called file cabinets, in the following manner: **One** for yourself, **one** for your wife, **one** for each of the children, **one** for your home, and **one** for your business. Now you may be thinking that you do not have a business. Well, assign one for a business anyway.

Acquire at least ten files for each of the drawer. More if you need them. Denote each one carefully, depending on what is the most important in your life. NOT what is *deemed* to be, or *supposed* to be, but that which *is* important to you.

For example, in my file cabinet, I have such files as "car pictures", and "writing". Do whatever pleases you, but do not ignore important matter, such as bills, and legal documents. In any case, assign at least ten files for yourself. Follow through in this manner for your wife, and the children. Taking care that you have enough folders to accommodate your work and children's school.

In the House cabinet, have files for matters that are common to everyone in the household, community subjects, and general house documents, such as mortgage information, utility statements, and common credit card bills. Basically, everything that cannot be classified as a personal matter.

For the Business cabinet, if you do not have a business, include anything and everything that you *wished* would be in there. For example, if you ever wanted to have your own flower shop, then put things such as listings for flower shop sales in the local newspaper. Or if you wanted to own your own airlines, then put sale advertisements of passenger jetliners in there.

This does not have to be very realistic as far as your logical mind is concerned, but you have to take special care that you do not put your current work matter in it. This cabinet is created to polish your "mind" organization, to help you carry your exercise in organization even further, by reaching for things that *do not exist* at the present moment, as well help you with your goal setting process.

If you have your own business, then create an extra cabinet, which will be designated as "extra" business, "better" business, "future" business, or whatever that excites you. This will be a vehicle for you to organize and refine your "mind" organization, as well as to propel you forward.

It has always been my belief that one must acquire the fundamentals of the core subject, before exploring the functional part of it. The fundamentals can be just learning the history, or be involved in some kind of a philosophical discussion of it. As in the case of Organization, everything that follows, no matter how little, or how large, is based on the fundamentals. And we just went through it in the last few pages.

THE ORGANIZATIONAL FLAVOR

So far our discussions about organization have taken a deductive reasoning route. We have gone from the somewhat abstract to the specific. So by using common sense, we can assume that we can continue on this direction and occupy every inch of our lives with organizational logic.

Using common sense, unfortunately, does not endorse that for us at all. Even to say that common sense is common would be in error.

Keeping that in mind, we then do not take it for granted that everything we do will have an organizational flavor to it. From the most basic things, such as organizing our desks in the most efficient and ergonomic style, to the structure of a group we are forming for this or that reason.

The operative initiatives here is to be aware, alert, and awake to thoughts that flow in your mind, and gently apply any resources you can marshal to the end result of the pure impression of organization.

The Life Management Schedule

I t may seem to some readers that we should have tackled the question of scheduling before we begin to implement any sort of methodology. The reality is quite the opposite, as the Life Management Schedule contains almost all the elements of Life Management. Particularly the following:

- Dates & Duration

- Tasks

- Resources

- Dependencies

- Baseline (Planned and Actual)

DATES, DURATION, AND TASKS

The Dates and Duration section deals with your idea of the project, for example, if it is a project that you would like to implement for buying a house, then you can very closely estimate the Date and Duration of the project, such as:

Dates: January 1st to March 15th

If it is an activity that you are planning, and it is in the future, especially those involving a future goal, then it is quite acceptable to have a loose estimation, for example:

Summer Vacation to Alaska: Summer of 2003 for six weeks.

Nevertheless, it is important to have an idea of the date and duration of the project or activity.

Once you have a Date and Duration estimation, then you must assign tasks, in conjunction to the duration of the project. It would be an obvious assumption, but let me just say that all your tasks must fall within the walls of the duration of the project. If the project's duration is from January 1st to March 15th, then all the tasks must fall between the dates January 1st to March 15th. The tasks are permitted to broaden beyond each other's boundaries, and overlap.

For example, in the Home Loan project, we had the following chronological breakdown:

Jan 1–Jan 15

Study the general neighborhood

Real Estate Agent contact

Acquire listings

See properties

Jan 16–Jan 31

Survey the price range

Research and analyze financial feasibility

Browse individual houses

Select house

Feb 1–Feb 15

Financial Agent contact

Real Estate Lawyer contact

Synchronize Real Estate Agent with Real Estate Lawyer and Financial Agent

Feb 16–Feb 28

Select house

Acquire credit report

Correct credit aberrations

Negotiate loan points

Communicate with Real Estate Lawyer of the selling party

Check property documentation

Contact inspector, appraiser, and movers

Mar 1–Mar 15

Inspect property

Appraise property

Deliver financing

Close on property

Coordinate with utilities

Secure city permits and formalities

Coordinate with the movers for move date

Conduct moving activities

The entries you see below for each of the timeline, are converted to individual tasks, and assigned a date. The tasks at this time may change a bit to reflect the correctness of newly acquired information. Remember that the task dates are not written in stone to mirror either the difficulty of accuracy of the event happening on a particular date, or the duration of the tasks. For example, the task to correct credit aberrations is given a normally accepted duration of 10 days, but in actuality it is quite difficult to estimate.

A suitable example could be as follows, you may also see how the separate components of the methodology can come together to serve a single purpose:

Jan 1–Jan 15

Study the general neighborhood—Jan 1st to Jan 3rd

Real Estate Agent contact—Jan 4th

Acquire listings—Jan 7th to Jan 10th

See properties—Jan 10th to Jan 15th

Jan 16–Jan 31

Survey the price range—Jan 16th to Jan 20th

Research and analyze financial feasibility—Jan 16th to Jan 31st

Browse individual houses—Jan 16th to Jan 31st

Select house preliminary—Jan 20th to Jan 31st

Feb 1–Feb 15

Financial Agent contact—Feb 1st

Real Estate Lawyer contact—Feb 1st

Synchronize Real Estate Agent with Real Estate Lawyer and Financial Agent—Feb 1st to Feb 15th

Feb 16–Feb 28

Select house final—Feb 16th to Feb 20th

Acquire credit report—Feb 16th

Correct credit aberrations—Feb 16th to Feb 26th

Negotiate loan points—Feb 16th to Feb 28th

Communicate with Real Estate Lawyer of the selling party—Feb 20th to Feb 28th

Check property documentation—Feb 20th to Feb 28th

Contact inspector, appraiser, and movers—Feb 16th to Feb 28th

Mar 1–Mar 15

Inspect property—Mar 1st

Appraise property—Mar 1st

Deliver financing—Mar 5th

Close on property—Mar 5th

Coordinate with utilities—Mar 5th to Mar 10th

Secure city permits and formalities—Mar 5th to Mar 10th

Coordinate with the movers for move date—Mar 5th to Mar 10th

Conduct moving activities—Mar 15th

The task assignment entries are a major accomplishment, as this signals a certain reality of the project actually happening. The excitement of the possibilities is realized even greatly, when resources are assigned responsibilities.

RESOURCES

The schedule takes a distinct shape, as each task is allocated a specific resource to get the job done. At this time, you can also make the decision as to the format of your schedule. You can keep it in the Work Breakdown Structure format, or if you are working with a paper and a pencil, and have a bigger space to work on, you can stretch the schedule horizontally, for example:

Jan 1–Jan 15----------Jan 16–Jan 31----------Feb 1–Feb 15----------Feb 16–Feb 28

Below each of these timelines, you can put the tasks and the resources, and ultimately, the rest of the components of the schedule. For this example, we will continue with the Work Breakdown Structure format.

As you prepare to assign the resource, you can assign a "Hard Name", or a "Soft Name". Hard Names are resources that have been identified, such as, Abe, Margie, or Honest Ed. Soft Names are those, which can be identified later, such as Resource 1, Resource 2, Resource 3. Or you can identify the Soft Names by their functions, such as Real Estate Lawyer. You can plug in the Hard Names at a later time.

Jan 1–Jan 15

Study the general neighborhood—Jan 1st to Jan 3rd—Abe

Real Estate Agent contact—Jan 4th—Margie

Acquire listings—Jan 7th to Jan 10th—Abe/Margie

See properties—Jan 10th to Jan 15th—Abe/Margie

Jan 16–Jan 31

Survey the price range—Jan 16th to Jan 20th—Abe

Research and analyze financial feasibility—Jan 16th to Jan 31st—Abe

Browse individual houses—Jan 16th to Jan 31st—Abe/Margie

Select house preliminary—Jan 20th to Jan 31st—Abe/Margie

Feb 1–Feb 15

Financial Agent contact—Feb 1st—Margie

Real Estate Lawyer contact—Feb 1st—Margie

Synchronize Real Estate Agent with Real Estate Lawyer and Financial Agent—Feb 1st to Feb 15th—Abe

Feb 16–Feb 28

Select house final—Feb 16th to Feb 20th—Abe/Margie

Acquire credit report—Feb 16th—Abe

Correct credit aberrations—Feb 16th to Feb 26th—Abe/Margie

Negotiate loan points—Feb 16th to Feb 28th—Abe/Margie

Communicate with Real Estate Lawyer of the selling party—Feb 20th to Feb 28th—Real Estate Lawyer

Check property documentation—Feb 20th to Feb 28th—Real Estate Lawyer

Contact inspector, appraiser, and movers—Feb 16th to Feb 28th—Abe

Mar 1–Mar 15

Inspect property—Mar 1st—Property Inspector

Appraise property—Mar 1st—Property Appraiser

Deliver financing—Mar 5th—Financial Agent/ Real Estate Agent

Close on property—Mar 5th—Real Estate Lawyer/ Real Estate Agent/ Abe/Marge

Coordinate with utilities—Mar 5th to Mar 10th—Abe

Secure city permits and formalities—Mar 5th to Mar 10th—Abe/ Real Estate Lawyer

Coordinate with the movers for move date—Mar 5th to Mar 10th—Abe

Conduct moving activities—Mar 15th—Movers/Abe/Marge

Do you see the skeletonized version of the Schedule taking the meat? The schedule, when finished, will be able to give you a comprehensive look at the whole project. We will continue now by adding the Dependencies, and finally adding the Baseline.

DEPENDENCIES AND BASELINE

Dependencies and Baseline are the last two components of the schedule that I work on, as I feel that I acquire a lot of knowledge from the process of getting to that point. I have a little bit more clarity of the project. In the world of the Professional Project Manager, dependencies can become enormously complicated, and they continue to become even more complex, as the number of projects run by that Project Manager increases.

In the Life Management methodology, we will confine the dependencies to the project, instead of across several projects. The main reason for that is the fact that life is not an assembly line of projects that you embark upon, but a way of dealing with those that are placed in front of you by life itself. Hence, we do not expect you to be involved in complex multiple projects, which share tasks.

In this case, for example, the "Acquire listings" task is dependent on the "Real Estate Agent contact" task. In other words, you cannot acquire the listing, without first contacting the Real Estate Agent. You can either document this dependency by drawing a line between the two tasks, or make a documentation of the dependency next to the task. For example:

Real Estate Agent contact—Jan 4th—Margie

Acquire listings—Jan 7th to Jan 10th—Abe/Margie (*task dependency on "Real Estate Agent contact"*)

Of course, the tasks do not have to be consecutive in sequence, as in the case above.

The baseline, on the other hand, is more of a learning process. With each project that you undertake, you get better in its execution, for even when the general parameters of the projects differ, the core methodology remain the same. To baseline is to create a plan, which you expect to meet initially.

In this example, we can consider the dates that we have assigned to the schedule. That is your baseline. Now as you execute the plan, you will notice that the dates will change. For example, the "Acquire credit report" task may not be exactly on Feb 16th, or the task of "Correct credit aberrations" may well take more then ten days.

And if you have a budget for the project, which depends on the task being executed, then the baseline can be of a great help. For example, if your baseline expect the appraisal of the house to take three hours, and you are paying the resource $150 an hour, then any shift in the baseline time will impact your budget.

These departures from the initial expectation must be recorded and documented, so in the future if you undertake similar projects, or execute similar tasks, you have a better understanding of the dynamics of the project mechanism.

To End it All

I t will never do anybody justice to simply put the information in front of the readers, and expect them to learn and execute the new philosophy, values, or methodology. It does not do justice to the designer of the idea, and it does not do justice to the receiver of the idea. In fact, it is quite unjust and unfair to society as a whole, which contains the designer and the receiver.

Look down the line of your own history, there are distinct stages of acceptance of new and revolutionary ideas. At first the terror embedded in humanity rejects it. Then the inquisitiveness in us learns from it. The ambitious and motivated practices it. The adjudicator in us judges it. And that is where it ends. Thousands of years can pass, or just moments. We stand at this final moment then, the new idea fatigued or exhausted by the process of these stages. We either forget about it, or the idea works its way in our natural consciousness.

When Copernicus's presented the world with the Copernican Theory, stating that the Sun, and not the Earth, was at the center of the universe, it was considered far-fetched and implausible by everyone. In fact, his work, "De revolutionibus orbium coelestium", which translates to "*On the revolutions of the heavenly spheres*", was not published till the very end of his lifetime.

Then the cycle started to spin, and we evolved to the second stage and started learning from it. Finally, notables like Galileo and Newton practiced it. Then the rest of the world fell in place, and now we do not even think otherwise. Of course, Copernicus had his Italians, Socrates had his Greeks, Voltaire had his French, and the history is full of them.

But they were not alone, nor they ever will be. In fact, the rite of genius is not reserved for geniuses. You and I are part of it also. You

171

and I also have our Italians, Greeks, and French. We all have ideas of different magnitudes and intensities, and parts of us all strive for acceptance, and excellence.

Our ideas presented in the last 100 years or so, have actually been fair to the human race. We have the privilege and opportunity to dissect, analysis, and digest the new ideas. They are not simply put in front of us, for us to either accept or reject them.

We credit this to the fact that we are more sophisticated as humans, and even more so, we are more tolerant.

But what is fair? The fact that the genius of the ancient time can put forth an idea in front of you and the intellects of the time, which amounted to a small number of people, can then decide whether to accept or reject the idea? Or the present time, where the mass can study and accept or reject an idea, whereby taking the risk of diluting it?

Certainly the present system gives us more freedom in the decision, but at the same time takes the risk of taking a genius idea and reducing it to a commercial pulp of mass appeal. It becomes the thirst quencher for the present intellectual needs.

But the privilege remains. We can pick and choose. And that privilege, that dispensation allowed to us by the evolution of humanity, is unique to our time. But this does not continue on forward from here. The hail of ideas, inventions, and discoveries has turned the exclusive exception of a new idea into a process of many proposals.

Hence, the only reasonable resolution to this dance of logic, humanity, genius, and discovery is the advancement of the process. The belief that in order to improve humanity, we must now improve the process, and thus become more efficient. This conviction has been reflected with conviction in the business world, and has steadily made its way in the daily activities of managers, and workers, in the form of methodology, guidelines, and procedures.

It remains to be seen if one embraces Perfect Life Management, thus becoming a Life Wizard, falls in the category of the same steps as some of the other great ideas of our time. But one thing rests in clarity, and that is the fact that this kind of Life Management makes life more efficient.

Perfect Life Management has to be appreciated in the fact that the methodology undertakes the bigger challenges of life, such as major purchases, but does not discriminate and discount the small details, which makes up the greater part of everyday living.

It maneuvers the major issues by setting a complete methodology mirroring the proven system of the corporate sphere. One can single out only a solitary exercise, such as meetings or status reports to undertake a particularly difficult area of life. Or deploy the whole compliment of Perfect Life Management to embark upon a major purchase, such as Work Breakdown Structure, Critical Path Method, and Budget & Risk Analysis.

Or simply, reflect on the philosophical and practical uses of Goal Manifestation, Organization, and Family Review.

A Life Wizard then is not only a metaphorical title, but also the ability of a mere human to transform to become a competent and resourceful machine. Perfect Life Management gives us reason, motive, and sometimes the sanity to pursue the daily activities of life with dignity and purpose. It is not claimed to be perfect, but certainly it can be claimed to be the perfect *pursuit* of creating a happy and effective life, and create value to friends and family.

Epilogue

We have a certain vision of the future, and we have a particular image of the past, but we make the present along as we live in it. The idea behind Perfect Life Management was initially to give the present a structure. But in the process of making the present a bit more efficient, we are offered a variety of derivatives, which categorically compliments the present, and at the same time, enhances the future and enlightens the past.

The present, of course, improves by deploying selected methodology. Having a distinct objective and purpose, as well, liberates the future. But it is the past, which is viewed with interest, when we see the documentation and the unambiguous record that is left behind by the Life Wizard. Some of us achieve this repute by forceful effort after studying methods and procedures, and some of us arrive by unconscious design. The way of arrival is irrelevant, because the end effect is the same.

As I grew up in several different countries, I had the biggest adventures of my life. I had comfort and opulence as a prevailing criterion, and not an exception. My early recollections of a train ride were of riding in the engine with the engineer, and not packed in the passenger berth. My initial memory of an airplane was one of meeting the Captain in the cockpit, and not stuffed in the cabin. My first reminiscences of life were of sumptuousness and extravagance, rather then a blend of featureless chronicles. In short, I had a privileged childhood.

But as I grew older I experienced a certain slippage in elation and delight of life. I realized that life was not all-exuberant events, but a series of ordeals, sprinkled with a few pleasures for precarious balance. The tragedy was that I actually believed it.

I did not have a system to look back and see what I had lost. It was not about wealth, that much I trusted life, but about the *system* of living. I knew that I had lost something. I was sure that I had left something behind. I did not have a clear indication or the articulation of what it was.

But as I practice Life Management, I assure myself that will never happen again. I do not think that it was a childish fantasy, as I have felt the perks of the same sensation of pleasures, which I felt as a child, during certain events of my life. They all have a pair of things in common, the ability to live life with efficiency, and having a clear definition of purpose.

That definition of purpose will keep you on as straight of a line as the universe will allow; so you may enjoy the rewards that efficiency and purpose gives you. All you have to do is *row* with intent. Remember, if you row, you will not drift.

Additional Note:

Life Management is more then just efficiency. It is about personal development. For information about a free newsletter and free seminars in your area, please visit us at:

<u>http://www.ajani.com/</u>

0-595-24496-3

www.ingramcontent.com/pod-product-compliance
Lightning Source LLC
Chambersburg PA
CBHW021601280526
45784CB00001BA/453